NONHUMAN ART

Leonel Moura
© 2015
arte@leonelmoura.com

Publisher
LxXL
lxxl@mail.telepac.pt

Graphic Design
Robotarium
arte@robotarium.pt

ISBN-13: 978-1514853344
ISBN-10: 1514853345

INTRODUCTION

I have seen an "Ant Algorithm" at work for the first time back in 1998. It was the version of Chialvo and Milonas after Marco Dorigo's "Ant System" proposed in his 1992 Ph. D. thesis. Running in a computer it seemed to me at first glance to have some similarities with Conway's "Game of Life". I saw the same grid of black and white cells, with black representing the ants and white the environment. But looking closer I understood that there was no resemblance at all. In reality the grid was not black and white but a shade of grey, i.e. with 256 possible states and what I called a grid was actually a bitmap. Ants where not defined by a black cell but alter the state of the cells that they cross.

The algorithm simulates the behavior of ants. A set of "ants" were launched haphazardly on a white bitmap environment (all pixels at 255). They start by moving randomly leaving a trail of "pheromone", which means changing the state of the pixels that they cross in one shade of grey for iteration. When other ant crosses this path it tends to follow it with a certain probability. After a while some trails emerge.

The original algorithm was created to demonstrate a probabilistic optimization method. However, as an artist, I didn't see ants or optimization, but rather a drawing being made by a process not entirely controlled by the human that triggered it. That is, a drawing created at least partially by a nonhuman entity.

In the first experiments I have used an interface, a CAD/CAM machine, connected to a computer running the ant algorithm. The trails of the "ants" were translated into a painting by the improvised robot arm. One of these first "swarm paintings" later appeared at the cover of the MIT magazine on Artificial Life.

But, although exciting, the exercise was not totally satisfying. There was still too much of a printing machine here. Hence I moved to real robots.

In 2003, with the help of a recently created robot company by IST (Technical Institute of Lisbon) graduates, we built 12 small robots looking and acting like artificial ants. As far as I know this was the first time that a swarm of robots was used to produce art works.

The initial paintings revealed that the robots didn't gener-

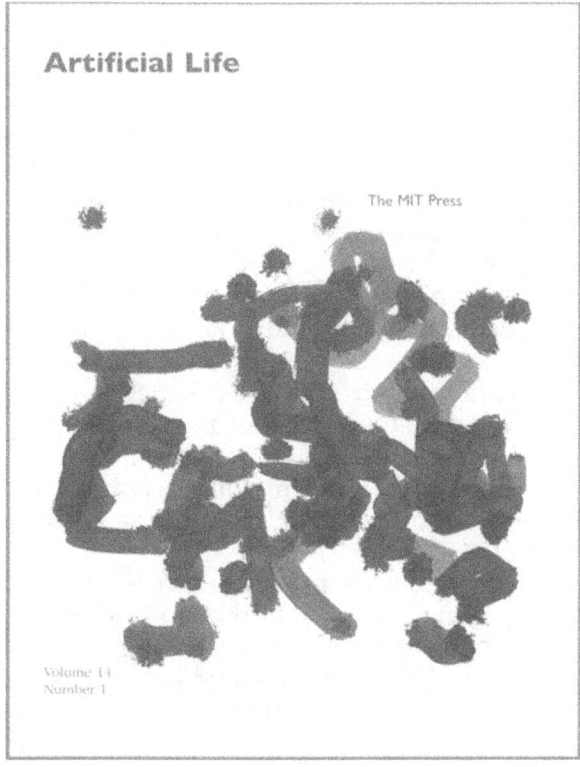

Artificial Life magazine cover, MIT Press, 2008

ate trails but clusters of color. In my model "pheromone" was replaced by color. If a certain amount of color was detected the robots tend to add more of the same range. Less than that amount the machine consider it to be still white and move ahead on its random walk.

When the decision was taken to add more color the robot activate one of the two available markers: the warm for yellows and reds and the cold for blues and greens. After a while, from a random background, a composition of color clusters was produced.

It was clear to me that although I made the robots, wrote the algorithm and trigger the process, the paintings were not entirely my making. Important information was gathered by the robots themselves, decisions were made on the basis of a stigmergic mechanism and a kind of collective heuristic behavior was at work. I coined it "nonhuman art".

The importance of this label can only be understood in the context of art evolution. Since Duchamp art is no longer the demonstration of manual skill, artisanal practice or the expression of a declarative intentionality. The "Ready-made" opened the door to all kind of manifestations: everything is possible if accepted by the art world.

The last century is therefore characterized by a constant expansion of what society is ready to accept as art, such as a gesture, the body of the artist, an idea, a social protest, a performance, a film or video or a pile of garbage. Piero Manzoni's "artist's shit" (1961), a tin can filled with his own feces, and the "Air conditioning show" by Art & Language (1967), an empty exhibition space with the air conditioning on, are extreme and singular examples.

For some artists making art mean to launch the question: are you ready for this? Are you ready to consider a urinal a work of art?

Critics, curators, Museum directors and collectors made and keep on making an enormous effort to give a transcendent significance to the successive collapse of art borders, unwilling to accept that the step from possible to impossible made possible is, often, what really matters in a particular art manifestation.

As an artist I inscribe my action in this process of enduring art expansion. Hence the question: are you ready for nonhuman art?

4

SYMBIOTIC ART MANIFESTO [2004]

1) Machines can make art
2) Man and machine can make symbiotic art
3) Symbiotic art is a new paradigm that opens up new ways for art
4) It involves totally relinquishing manufacture and the reign of the hand in art
5) It involves totally relinquishing personal expression and the centrality of the artist/human
6) It involves totally relinquishing any moralist or spiritual ambition, or any purpose of representation

[Making the Artists that make the Art]

Art as we know it is dead. This time it is definite and official.

Often declared during the last century though never actually achieved, the death of art is now a fact. Not just out of a mere wish or avant-garde rhetoric, but because the conditions for artistic production have changed brusquely. Suddenly, all of modern art has become ancient art. Because the idea of art as a product exclusively of human creativity has been finally abandoned, to adopt the notion that it is the direct output of non-human artists.

As usual, such a change of paradigm has only been possible through technological evolution. From the analysis of the parts we move on to the mechanics of complexity. By studying living organisms we are now in a position to realize life as it could be.

When robots ceased to merely simulate human behavior, such as walking, playing football or cracking jokes, to start being used to make art, something very radical happened. Robots that make art are not only questioning the idea of art or philosophy, they even cast doubts on our own condition as human beings. Why bother continuing to do something that machines can do better and more consistently? If art has no purpose, as all the modern and post-modern theories declare, then machines are the best creators.

6   *Portrait generate by the "Ant Algorithm", 2001*

Once having freed ourselves from making art we may now devote our efforts to generate a new type of artist born from the broth of protobiotics, robotics and artificial life. We can build the machines that will make art. This new artist/machine has no predetermined objective, nor aesthetics, morals or intent. He realizes the last of the "pure psychic automatism" as announced by Breton and partly developed by Pollock. Besides, there is no concern about individualism or identity. The action is collective and the World is apprehended as a common territory emerging from a stigmergic behavior.

From a philosophical standpoint the action is relational and the works that are generated are synthetic proposals issuing from the unraveling of collective experimentation. The life of the artist/machine is interlinked to the life of the artist/human.

When we cease to make art to start making artists, what do we become ourselves? We become symbiotic artists! Humans are no longer concerned about the direct production of objects, but dedicate all their knowledge and energy to create and co-operate with an imaginary, non-human life that is devoted to art-making.

In doing so, the symbiotic artist asserts that technology serves creativity and not the destructive military industry or mercantilism.

The role of the symbiotic artist from now on is to create non-human artists and to cooperate with them to produce art. This entails understanding the rudiments of non-anthropocentric life and creating the conditions for experimentation to take place. In other words, art as it could be. Art of the 21st Century.

LEONEL **MOURA**

THE ISTANBUL MANIFESTO [2011]

Marcel Duchamp's idea was to make art with the already made.

Our idea is to make art that makes art.

Manufacturing is obsolete. Manual skill leads only to a senseless waste of time. The human artist is not a maker, but a creator. Art is a mind extension, a prosthetic, a machine that just waits to be triggered. The role of the artist is to push the ON button, giving rise to an autonomous product.

Art is fundamentally biological and evolutionary. Art is everywhere. Each life form generates a particular kind of art that spreads from simple patterns to complex symbolic communication. Organisms use chemicals, odors, touch, sounds and vision to produce art. Termites build mud structures; birds make colorful installations; whales sing. Humans assemble machines. These machines produce new designs, elaborate forms and compose images. They play music, dance and perform. Soon they will engender astonishing ideas and have futuristic visions. How can a human artist keep on making drawings, paintings or sculptures with his own hands? How can anyone still believe that art is an exclusive human feature?

A new kind of art is emerging out of proto-artificial life forms. These new artificial organisms are biological in essence. Some have tissues, some mechanical parts and others a combination of both. They think and create. Soon they will reproduce and evolve without human intervention. They will be entirely autonomous. The role of the human artist is to give birth, to activate, to let it go, to lose control. We can make the artists that make the art.

Isn't it a marvelous sensation to see a machine creating a painting on its own? To show, before our eyes, a competence

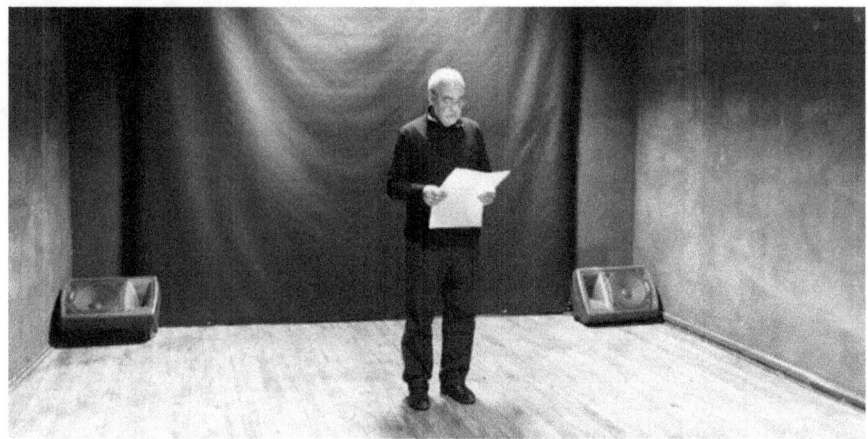

Launched at Galata Perform, Istanbul, April 7, 2011

that our ancestors thought to be exclusively human? Isn't such a painting the most amazing art work since the first cave etchings? Isn't it the superb output of a freshly arrived intelligence on earth?

Art is everywhere. Natural life do it. Artificial life do it too. Art is beyond humankind . How can we be insensitive to this extraordinary proliferation of creativity? Why be fearful of what adds, doesn't subtract? How not embrace enthusiastically this non zero sum game?

Human artists are part, not the whole. Human artists can make a difference by exploring the full extension of creativity.

The great artist of tomorrow will not be human.

LEONEL **MOURA**

SOCIAL FICTION INTERVIEW [2002]

Social Fiction
We encountered the research of Leonel Moura with nonhu-
man art or 'swarm paintings' though a posting on the Rhizome
e-mail list. Because we liked his work to create art with ma-
chines we decided to e-mail him some questions. Here are the
answers:

Can you tell me something about your background & how
you became interested in complexity / a-life?

Although my main activity is art, I have always been interested in architecture, politics, philosophy and science. One
of the consequences of these broad interests is my regular involvement with the organization of events and conferences putting art and science together.

In 1997 the government asked me to conceive a Pavilion for
the World Fair in Lisbon Expo'98. Task that includes architecture
and content. The government idea was to represent the region-
al and traditional Portugal, but I have been able to change it and
to create a space entirely dedicated to innovation. To achieve
this I have looked for the most advanced research in my country and, in one of my visits to a lab meet a scientist working
with alife. I did know something about genetic algorithms, but
not much about swarm intelligence. I was fascinated and from
there we start to collaborate.

Can you tell me some more what you're work/research was
about which leaded you to your current swarm paintings. Are
there any examples on-line

My objective is to create a model to test the emergence
of collective intelligence in human groups. The swarm paintings are just an experimental step with implications in the art
problematic. My idea is to show these paintings in a Gallery or
Museum and not so much in the net, exactly to avoid the lack of
materiality when we see them in a monitor.

NONHUMAN ART

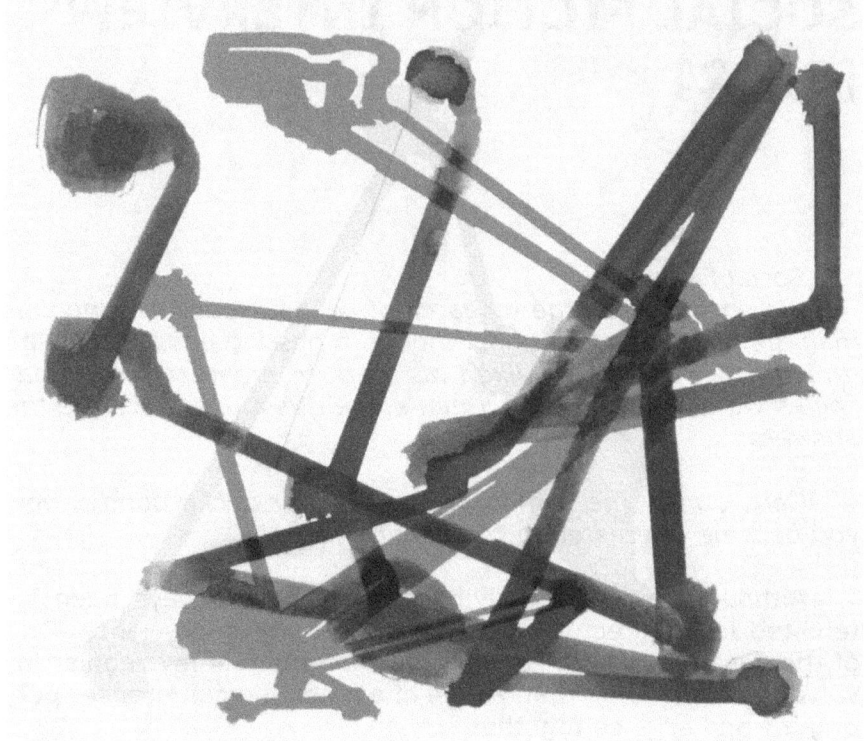

Swarm painting, 021, 2002, acrylic on paper, 30 x 33 cm

Your current research is about non-human painting aka swarm paintings. What's so fascinating about it?

Art is for too long concerned with form. I believe it is time to change to mechanism. Therefore it is not important to be hand-made. On the contrary, it is more interesting if it is machine made, be it a robot or a colony of virtual ants. The designation nonhuman art is provocative but also factual, because these paintings are the product of a small but autonomous intelligence. At most we have create the artist, but not the art.

What technology do you use & how? do you use already available technology or do you develop your own? is this important to you?

These experiments are based on "ant algorithms". In this

kind of research the technology is many times the target itself.

Basically the model conditions are:

We create an environment and drop artificial ants.

It is assumed that each organism emits pheromone at a given rate, and there is no spatial diffusion. Also global pheromone evaporates after all ants have moved at a given rate.

The ants are not allowed to have any memory and the individual's spatial knowledge is restricted to local information about the pheromone density.

The pheromonal field (cognitive map) contains information about past movements and decisions of the organisms, but not arbitrarily far in the past since the field "forgets" its distant history due to evaporation in time.

Toroidal boundary conditions are imposed on the lattice to remove, as far as possible, any boundary effects.

Nonlinear response or directional bias is introduced in order to form trails, or to persist on past trails that are already formed.

Thus the paintings in fact reproduces, with the help of a robot, the pheromone trails at a given iteration (time). More pheromone more paint.

As an artist you use science to let art emerge outside your own control. What are your main objectives with this? to create new forms? to protest against the art-maffia & their doctrines of originality? to show something? to gain insight on what's the difference of being man instead of monkeys or machine? or otherwise.

In art we live under the Duchamp's paradigm. Basically it means that the object is not very important, it is its relation with a specific place that matters. Thus this paradigm suggests already a simple mechanism of emergence. By displacing an object from one place to another, both the object and the context change, and through this art emerges.

I want to go further. I want to introduce stigmergy.

Stigmergy is an indirect communication through the environment. It works like this. One agent changes the environment and by that creates a stimulus for other agents to keep on changing. They don't relate to each other and don't follow any previous plan.

Duchamp's paradigm is not dynamic. After all, once the object gains its new place it becomes just another art object. Untouchable and static. On the contrary, I want to introduce

NONHUMAN ART

interactivity in a multi agent environment. The art milieu is a good place to do it.

The use of the word swarm suggests the existence of a colony that acts to our perception as one entity, how does this translate in your work?

The paintings are the product of the colony, not of the individual ants. The model is based on stigmergy. The deposition of pheromone by one ant stimulates more deposition from other ants. The global map is essentially holistic.

Should art be regarded as more than images alone? are the personal history of the artist, the place of the artwork in art history, the interpretation of a artwork that the artist give, not as much part of what defines interesting art as the art itself? How does this socially constructed value of art tie in with your objectives with swarm painting?

Art for me are not images, nor forms. Art is a cultural behavior, i.e. a human concept, involving artists, but also, curators, critics, collectors, public and anyone that, in a way or another, is related to it. This collective behavior produces a kind of pheromone trails that work as a stimulus to all agents.

When we look at culture as a pheromone map everything becomes clear. Some works have a high level of pheromone deposition, because many people like them, and thus it attracts more and more concentration of pheromone. The same with, for example, Museums or other cultural buildings. The social value of art is not the result of anyone decision in particular, or institution approval, but emerges from a complex and intricate collective behavior.

What are your plans for the future? which direction will your work take?

I am starting to work with robotics. I feel the need to give a body to the ant swarm.

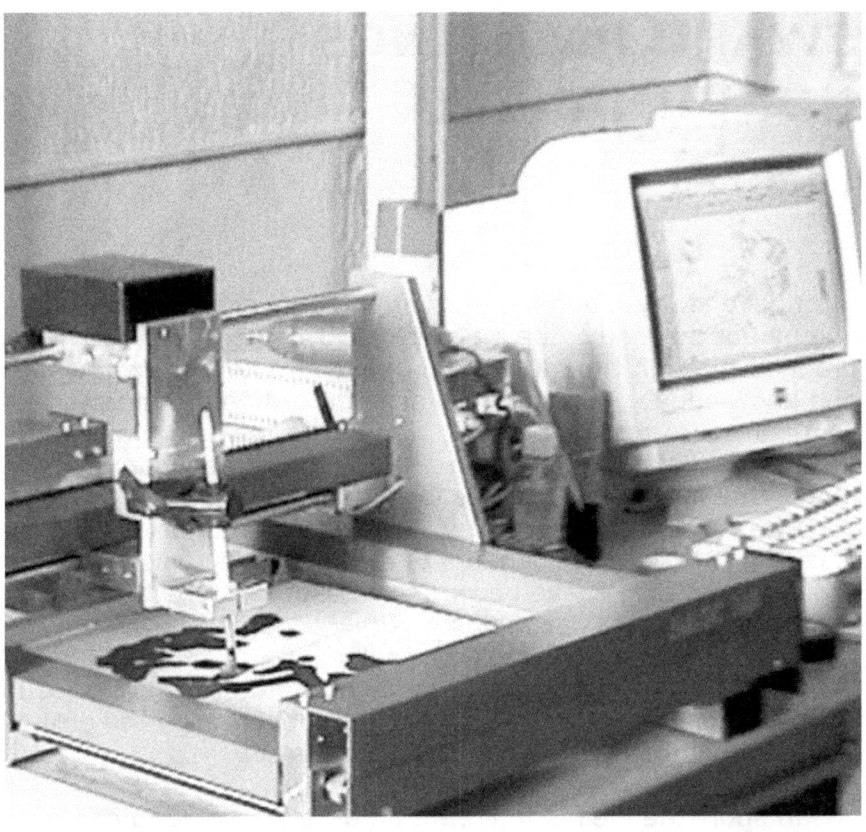

Computer running an ant algorithm connected to a (CAD/CAM) robotic arm as painting device, 2002

SWARM PAINTINGS
NONHUMAN ART
[2002]

14 I have always searched outside the art world the intellectual stimulation needed to be an artist, as I belief that creativity is produce through the interaction between different experiences and knowledge's. This personal attitude as been reinforced in a context where artistic practices tended to rely more and more in self-referential and circular systems, very dependent of the mercantile interests, and thus loosing excitement and novelty.

I was lucky to feel in that way, because from the side of science the "artistic" components of artificial intelligence (AI) and artificial life (aLife) have become increasable interesting, giving birth to completely new fields of knowledge and new ideas regarding life, art and intelligence itself.

From this context were born several projects developed in collaboration with Vitorino Ramos and more recently the project of UnManned Art with Henrique Garcia Pereira.

In short the idea is to create an organism able to generate forms without any representational pre-commitment and with a minimum of esthetical intervention from our part. This project differs from others, namely those of algorithmic or evolutionary art, where purely random choices and/or an aesthetic fitness evaluation must be incorporated, with or without the requirement of pre-constraints. Such experiments are based on a kind of ideal form, determined directly by humans or developed by computers after learning human idiosyncrasies. It differs also from certain proposals of AI, which try to simulate representations, emotions or human sensitivity.

It is undeniable the interest of such experiments, but that is not the purpose of our project. We want to remove, as much as possible, the human factor. Particularly in what concerns aesthetic or ethical subjectivity, taste or style, leaving to the "artificial artist" the task to define its own "art". It is our intent to depreciate the quality of the 'oeuvre d'art', liberating the aesthetic experience from all the moralistic and individualistic mythologies. For that purpose we are working with "artificial ant systems" and "swarm systems".

LEONEL **MOURA**

This said, I must start by confessing some incredulity and frustration during the first year of work. Although we reached very quickly some fascinating results, it was difficult for me to perceive the utility of the exercise. As an artist, I asked often: 'yes it is nice, but what can I do with it?' Typically I was looking at artificial life as a new tool, capable of serving by means of its extraordinary combinatory performance my one specific objective. In fact I wanted those systems to perform tasks or solve problems. From that attitude and period I have accomplished some curious artistic and architectural projects, but not a new kind of art. Besides that the overwhelming images that appeared in the screen of the monitor, soon gave place to a feeling of inconsequence in practical terms. Because an artist is essentially a builder, of objects or situations, the virtual reality of the pixel universe appears as an insurmountable obstacle.

It didn't seem possible to undertake any significant conceptual or esthetical rupture by means of flickering digital images, for very complex and elaborate that they would be. As we can already state by looking at exhibitions and art magazines, contemporary art very soon did integrate such images, in the old logic of fashion and formalism.

The computer, primordial soup of the artificial life, is very deceptive when it comes to output. In the monitor all the images, reduced to their condition of pixels, seem similar and equivalent. Over and over again I initiate the program, drop a set of "ants" randomly in a delimited space (ambient) and witness the emergence of a variety of drawings, lines or clusters, mappings or 3d constructions, depending on the characteristics of the program or the specific parameters and grammar. The result was always exciting, and more exciting when increasing unexpected, that is, less controlled. But the monitor kept on returning this excitement to a kind of virtual dullness.

It was thus that after a sleepless night, I decided to break with the monitor and undertake a simple experiment. With the aid of a small CAD/CAM machine and a Japanese brush deepen in paint, I redirected the swarm to a white sheet of Fabriano paper. A painting emerged, formally similar to post-war abstract art, a children's drawing or the experiments with the chimpanzee Congo. I decide to call it "Swarm Paintings".

This first painting was a true revelation. Facing the naive scrabbles from the swarm, I felt to be in the presence of a conceptual shift. Those kind of things that creates a before and an after. The excitement changed into vision.

The following step, very laborious and complicated, was to

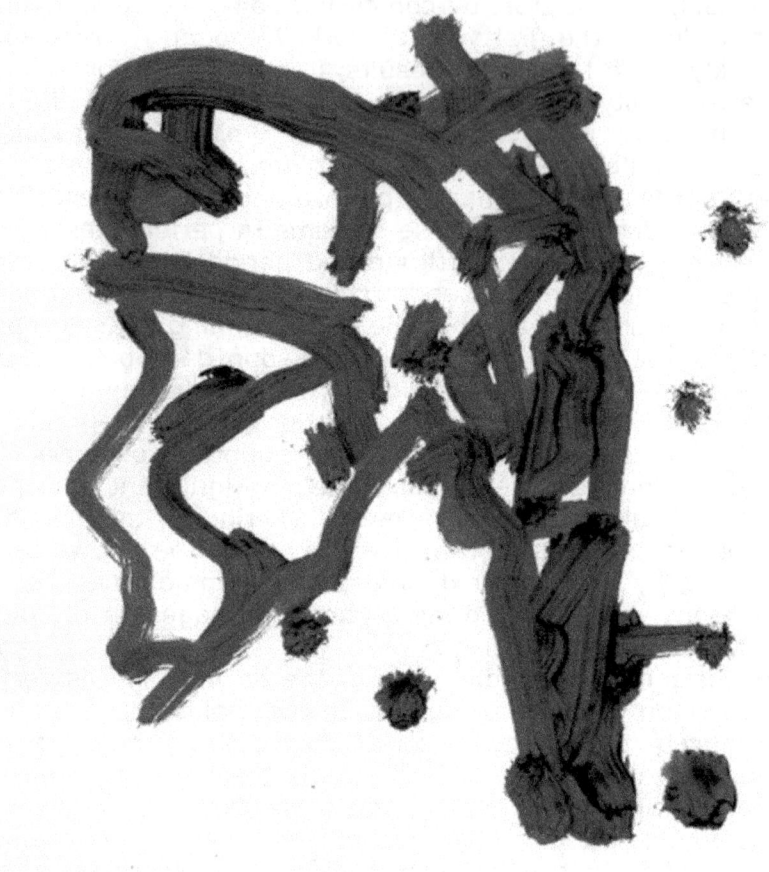

Swarm painting, 012, 2002, acrylic on paper, 40 x 33 cm

try to limit to the maximum the human intervention. Not only to bind the swarm directly with the painting machine, but also to increase autonomy at the level of the bottom-up methodological design. As a natural step I am now working with robotics.

The paintings and drawings reproduced here are the result of this "primitive" work. The colors and the formats are still my "interpretation". Actually in this first stage all the works from the artificial swarm are human assisted. But they will be less and less as the autonomy improves.

Anyway, it can already be stated that these "paintings" have very few human characteristics. They do not share practically any of the conditions of (human) authorship. They do not refer to a pre-committed representation, don't assume any sentimental pretension or express a particular sensibility, and moreover they don't expect an esthetical or ethical recognition. They also don't reveal taste, style or any message. They are a form of automatism at its most radical manifestation.

The similarities with recognized art works are due to the production context. That is, they are defects and not qualities, inevitable at this experimental phase where my intervention is still considerable. The more I will withdraw from it, the bigger the autonomy will grow. Tomorrow we will be able to "give birth" to an artificial life entirely dedicated to its "art".

The use of current artistic categories, such as drawings, paintings, sculptures, is not relevant to the process, but is justified by the need of a strategy of recognition for the art world, without which it would not be possible to introduce the questions that really matter.

The desire to gain autonomy is not new in art history. Three moments, corresponding to important aesthetical ruptures, are of particular importance. The use by Renaissance painters of the "Camara Obscura"; the "invention" of the abstraction in the beginning of 20th century; and, a little later, the appearance of the "ready-made" by Duchamp.

The "Camara Obscura" was not the first "machine" to help artists, but it embodies a fundamental moment, when in a conscientious and objective way an instrument of mediation between the model and its representation was adopted. By that it was possible to depreciate the subjective aspects of craftsmanship, allowing a concentration on the content. The invention of the "Camara Lucida" and later the photography has contributed decisively to radicalize the process. For example, Vermeer paintings would not be possible without the use of a "Camara Obscura". They look like Polaroid's, because they are in fact human assisted photographic snapshot.

If the "Camara Obscura" helped to concentrate on representation, the abstraction finally freed the artist from it. The art didn't need anymore to represent a portion of the reality, it become a reality on its own. The subject of art became art itself.

With Duchamp and his "ready-made" it was the statute of the work of art to be questioned. It didn't matter anymore the esthetical achievement, nor the skill of the author. The spectator and the context made the art. All the art after Duchamp is

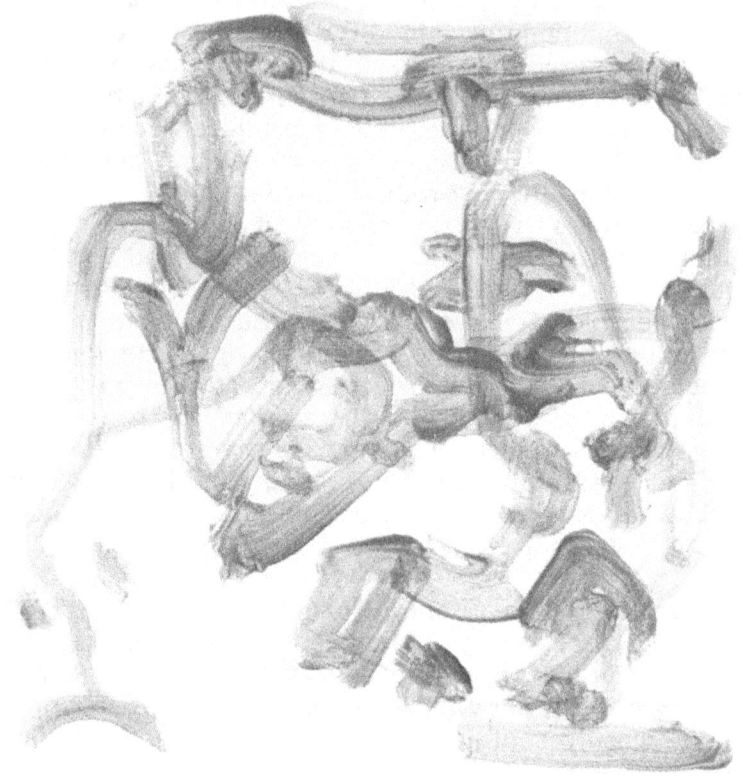

Swarm painting, 004, 2002, acrylic on paper, 33 x 33 cm

a context art, varying only in modalities of contextualization, decontextualization, recontextualization and so on.

At a first glance we can see these paintings as one particular way of output, to be considered in the same plane of an image in the monitor, a print, a digital photography or a video.

However the essence of these paintings is not in the image, but in the process. Its implications have little to do with the step from virtual to real, even if that is important in itself, but with the consequences that this *new art* will have in culture and society.

It is thus important to understand that we are not speaking about a machine that paints more or less randomly. A robot, with wheels or legs, that evolves on a surface by chance or based on a predetermined set of instructions. In this context let me play tribute to the unjustly forgotten Italian artist Pinot-Gallizio. Inventor of the "pittura industriale" he created a machine (human assisted) that spread energetically paint on rolls of canvas, later to be sold by the meter at the more appraised Art Galleries of the fifties.

Anyway swarm paintings are not simple mechanic automation. Randomness or combinatorial aspects are not relevant. In fact, these works emerge from artificial ants, through a process of deposition/evaporation of pheromone. Some draw trails (where more pheromone, means more paint), others define clusters or build 3d objects. The result is a cognitive map and not a mere mechanical pattern.

When we look at one of these paintings, with its own materiality, we are not in the presence of chance. We see the plastic expression of an (artificial) life form. "Swarm paintings" are the product of an ant-swarm system capable of registering its existential activity, in a delimited ambient and during a certain period of time. Each painting, drawing or sculpture represents the global behaviour of a set of agents in a bottom-up approach.

It is certain that we still need somebody and a context to disclose these works. This particular "artificial artist" depends, not only of human assistance, but also of a curator and probably also a dealer. But in the "swarm art" the essential decisions for the emergence of the forms belong entirely to the ant-swarm. Therefore this "art" cannot be attributed solely to any human being, even not to the author of the algorithm. That is, the programmer creates the "DNA" of the "artist", but not the art works. The true artist is the swarm.

The notion of life in the label *artificial life* attained a vast consensus in contemporary science. The life from aLife share a significant number of characteristics that are recognized as defining life itself. Morphogenesis, the ability to generate forms, reproduction, the capacity to transmit genetic information and therefore survive death, evolution the ability to adapt to a changing environment. Autopoiesis, the process whereby an organization produces itself, is another and more difficult to perform feature of life. "A physical system if autopoietic is living. In other words, we claim that the notion of autopoiesis is necessary and sufficient to characterize the organization of living systems." (Maturana & Varela) If we want to call art to the production of an artificial being than we must demonstrate to be in the presence of an autopoietic system. And that is the actual target of our undertaking. But from the moment we accept life in artificial life, there is no reason why not to call art to artificial art.

Richard Dawkins states that the difference between human art or design and the extraordinary forms that we encounter in nature, is due to the fact that the first are born from a mental project, while the second result from natural selection. Cultural and natural selection are supposed not to work in the same way.

However, art and culture is the result of historical and social consensus, established through a non analytical process. It is the community involved with the production, circulation and fruition of art that determines the value of a particular work of art or artist. Art that nobody is interested in faints, the one that pleases to a great number prospers and occupies the Museums and the collective imaginary. And, such as in nature, a bizarre mutation rejected first can in certain circumstances give place to a future consensus. Think about Van Gogh. This means that art and culture emerges also from a kind of "natural" selection.

The separation between *artistic forms* produced by nonhuman life, be it natural or so called artificial, and those made by human artists, is not justified. The extreme anthropocentrism that characterizes our culture is not clever, nor productive. The nature is bursting with extraordinary works of art that we should appreciate, as such, in order to enrich our environment and existences. The esthetical experience is present everywhere and it is not an exclusively human behaviour. For example beauty, so important for any definition of human aesthetics, can be translated as the level of adaptation of an organism to its environment. A greater beauty (or fitness) means a superior capacity of survival and reproduction. Thus to refuse all the possible forms, be it human mind origin, mechanical origin or natural selection origin, results in a limitation of our own universe. When our Museums will have human artefacts aside with nonhuman art (organic or artificial) the process of human aesthetic evolution will speed up. The development of forms will be more complex and dynamic. Typically self-centred subjective matters, as authorship, sensibility or taste, will tend to be irrelevant. The recognition that life, intelligence and art are everywhere will open a new vision of all things and reorient our own place in the universe. It will be less grandiloquent but much more productive and exciting.

TRAILS, ANTS AND STIGMERGY
[2002]

Trails

Whoever has walked through the countryside, whether wandering for fun or traveling by necessity, has undoubtedly at some time taken a trail that existed before, trails blazed by who knows whom. Some, if they are often used, are highly visible because no vegetation grows on them; others, in grassier or less often used areas, show slight traces of preview footsteps, barely sufficient to serve as orientation. In any case, we are less interested here in the configuration, consistency, or even quality of these trails, as in how they are generated. In most cases, they appear out of necessity, linking places or towns, and, naturally, the idea is either to make them as short or as safe as possible, or to follow the most scenic route. Essentially, therefore, the formation of a trail is a question of optimization. But since we are discussing trails that were not designed by any engineering or architecture firm, but which arose spontaneously in the countryside, this problem cannot be resolved globally. In reality, the problem is not even understood as such, but rather the result of a chaotic, non-lineal process.

In a first phase, different pathways arise at random. As more people walk through the area they gradually add increasingly efficient alternatives, here finding a shorter way, there an easier one. Over the course of time the earliest pathways, since they are no longer used, begin to disappear, once again becoming overgrown with grass, fading away by the work of nature. The trail emerges, then, both due to the traces left behind by all of those walking boots, and to the disappearance from lack of use, of less interesting alternatives. At any given moment, the trail is the result of a collective, unplanned action's impact on the environment. Moreover, the great majority of those who, with their footsteps, create these trails do not communicate among themselves, do not establish any kind of plan, nor do they previously define rules of behavior. They do not know each other, and often do not even care to do so. They all simply act upon a given environment, using elements that the environment itself provides for them.

In its apparent triviality, this example of trail-blazing serves to show that it is possible to draw up the map of a territory in a way very different from the conventional method. Without the benefit of any cartographic tools, a map arises out of the environmental experience itself.

Ants

In ants, trail formation is based on a process of deposition and evaporation of pheromones. These pheromones are made out of a chemical element, a kind of a scent, which simultaneously has the property of being agreeable to the ants - that is, to stimulate them - and that of being able to fade away over time.

The deposition of pheromones is an easily understood phenomenon, since it functions like Ariadne's thread in the Minotaur's labyrinth. An ant wandering about at random leaves behind a trail which enables to find the way back to the nest. However, should the ant find food, it will go back by the same trail depositing more pheromones and thus making the trail more clear-cut. Any ants passing by will find a stimulus stronger than their own trails, and soon they will all merge into one of those troops of hundreds or thousands of ants that we see so often. Meanwhile, the trails with a lower level of pheromone, to which no other insect has returned, disappear; that is, they evaporate. This is very important in terms of optimization. Let us suppose that the aforesaid ant troop was following a trail that was not the shortest route between the nest and the food. And then a single, less obsequious ant (because a stimulus is just a stimulus and not an order) finds a shortcut.

Two things happen: on this route the pheromone deposition is higher, and on the other, which takes longer to travel, pheromone evaporation is quicker. Then some ants begin to prefer the new route, and soon thereafter they perceive that the shortcut is more stimulating.

This process of pheromone deposition/evaporation, which represents a kind of environmental computation, really creates a kind of map very different from the ones with which we humans are familiar. In social insects, who draw their spatial memories on the environment the map is collective; it is not inside the head of any individual. In other words, there is no centralized control, no predetermined plan, no command. Everything happens through simple, individual, local behaviors, able to collectively produce a general behavior. Moreover, ants do not directly communicate among themselves. They do so through a message deposited in the environment; i.e., indirectly. The pheromone deposited by an individual has an effect on the activity of another individual. This process has been given the name "stigmergy", from the Greek stigma, mark, and ergon, work.

Engaging in some intellectual fantasy, we can say that it is as if reading a book provided us with an unavoidable stimulus to write another book, and so on. Actually, this is not such a bad example, because very probably our cultural production functions in this way. For some people, ideas are exciting, and lead to the appearance of new ideas (1). An aesthetic experience affects us so much that we feel impelled to paint a picture, too.

Stigmergy comprises a mechanism that, in collective terms, leads to the appearance of a map made by all of the agents involved. Ant trails emerge, they are not the result of a previous plan, or an order, or any kind of intentional act. Each ant really does nothing more than act on her own limited, local scale, without ever perceiving the map that appears as a result. But although each individual lacks this capacity, the colony seems to act as a whole. This is so much the case that the swarm can be seen as an independent entity, a higher level of life, possessing a collective intelligence (2).

Computers

The simplicity of these mechanisms enables us to easily transpose them to the world of computers, contributing to the resolution of many complex problems, and introduced a new vision of complexity itself.

Today, virtual ant colonies are used in multiagent systems, such as the Internet or mobile phones, or which require self-organizational capacities, as in robotics. However, their scope is much wider than that. We now have models that are able to explain individual and crowd behaviors in human beings, social organization or cultural evolution. Or things as difficult to quantify as taste or consensus.

These models are tested and simulated in computers.

In 1995, Dante Chialvo and Mark Millonas (3) stemming

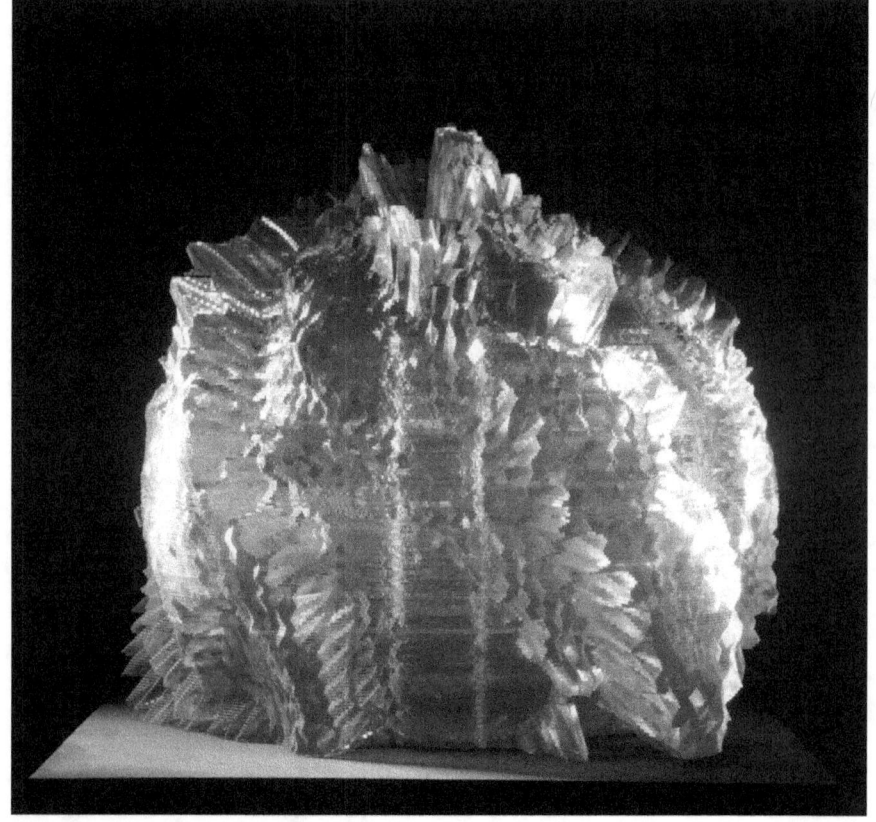

Swarm sculpture 2000, plexiglas, ø82 cm
physical translation of the pheromone peaks

from Marco Dorigo's first ant algorithm presented an version ble to reproduce the behavior of ant colonies in trail formation. Essentially, the algorithm simulates ant perception, movement through the environment, a capacity to recognize pheromones (stimuli) and to deposit it, as well as accumulation and evapo-ration over time (iterations). The pioneering experiment was conducted in a monochromatic environment i.e. without any previous stimuli. Even so, out of nothing, and after a few itera-tions, a collective map emerged.

We should highlight that both the pheromone trails and the resulting map are based, in the computers, on levels of grey. In reality, each ant alters the pixel level where it passes. To simpli-fy further: darker means more pheromone, lighter means less.

The environment of these ants can thus be seen as a landscape with mountains and valleys, filled with very high peaks and very low canyons.

In 1996, based on the model by Chialvo and Millonas, Vitorino Ramos (4) developed a new idea and created a new algorithm. Instead of working on a monochromatic base, he decided to introduce an image. In one of these experiments, we set loose a (virtual) ant colony onto an image of Kafka's face. In other words, a stimulated landscape.

The colony adapted to this environment, creating a cognitive interpretation of it. But then, after a few iterations, Kafka's face was removed, and substituted by an image of a red ant head. Something like pulling the rug out from under someone's feet, and replacing it with another one with a different design pattern. In the following iterations, Kafka's face remained as a sort of memory of the colony, until it gradually adapted to the new image. This memory, shared by all the ants, introduced a higher-level dynamic into the model. Something that, implicitly, we can call culture.

Stigmergy

Paths in the woods, ant trails, and their respective artificial models are based on the same mechanism that we are trying to understand here: stigmergy. The concept was introduced by Pierre-Paul Grassé (5) at the end of the 1950s, in studies that he carried out on social insects, to describe a particular form of indirect communication among individuals. It can be defined as a particular example of environmental or spatial synergy. The alteration of an environment by an individual sparks a stimulus in other individuals who, in turn, tend to intervene in (and modify) this environment. Termites use this mechanism to build their enormous clay cathedrals.

In the first phase, the insects randomly deposit little balls of clay impregnated with pheromone. The formation of a pile stimulates other termites to add more clay, and the higher the piles, the greater the stimulus. Little mounds are abandoned. Some columns grow and come together until they touch, forming arches. The result is an intricate and very solid structure.

As we can see, this system can be applied both to cooperation mechanisms in animals and to urban, social, cultural or political phenomena. The formation of cities is based, to a large extent, on processes of self-organization and stigmergy. Streets, houses, squares appear as the result of a construction/destruction process in a constant give-and-take of interests and expectations, the products of individual actions and of temporary collective consensus. Even when we consider planning and political decision-making, the development of a city, as a whole, results from the activity of multiple agents, all of whom act on a local level. In a wider context, the cities themselves can be seen, for the human race, as high peaks of social pheromone (stimuli) able to attract everything and everyone around them. In cultural production, there is also a clear stigmergetic effect. The cultural pheromone is a simultaneously quantitative and qualitative stimulus. In other words, in culture we never start from a monochromatic environment; on the contrary, whatever approach we take, we will always have an environment loaded with memory (pheromone peaks). From this point of view, contemporary cultural production is characterized by the reinforcement of certain trails and the abandoning of others, in a permanent reconstruction of the collective cognitive map.

This model's interest clearly resides in the fact that, for the first time, it is possible to understand cultural evolution without the need to emphasize moral or ideological concepts, aesthetics or ethics, beauty or intentionality.

[1] Tarde, Gabriel (1890) Les lois de l'imitation (2001) Les Empêcheurs de penser en rond, Paris

[2] Bonabeau E., M. Dorigo, G. Théraulaz. Swarm Intelligence: From Natural to Artificial System s. Santa Fe Institute in the Sciences of the Complexity, Oxford University Press, New York, Oxford, 1999.

[3] Chialvo, Dante R., Millonas, Mark M. "How Swarms Build Cognitive Maps" . In Luc Steels (Ed.), The Biology and Technology of Intelligent Autonomous Agents , (144) pp. 439-450, NATO ASI Series, 1995.

[4] Vitorino Ramos, Filipe Almeida, Artificial Ant Colonies in Digital Image Habitats - A Mass Behaviour Effect Study on Pattern Recognition, Proceedings of ANTS'2000 - 2nd International Workshop on Ant Algorithms (From Ant Colonies to Artificial Ants), Marco Dorigo, Martin Middendorf & Thomas Stüzle (Eds.), pp. 113 - 116, Brussels, Belgium, 7 - 9 Sep. 2000.

[5] Grassé, P. - P. "La Reconstruction du nid et les Coordinations Inter-Individuelles chez Bellicositermes Natalensis et Cubitermes sp. La théorie de la Stimergie: Essai d'interprétation du Comportement des Termites Constructeurs" Insect Soc. 6 (1959): 41 - 80

SYMBIOTIC ART
[2004]

Applications of collective robotics

Mankind has been intrigued by the possibility of 'building' artificial manlike creatures from the earliest times. For the ancient Greeks this possibility was provided by techné, the procedure that Aristotle conceived to create what nature finds impossible to achieve. Hence, under this view, techné sets itself up between nature and humanity as a creative mediation.

But 'machinism' became an object of fascination when vitalist conceptions assimilate machines to living beings, and a whole historical 'bestiary' of things related to machines stretches back centuries.

In the Hebrew tradition, the well-known Golem is an artificially created being made out of mud. If we move to Athens, the other 'pillar' of civilization as we know it, we find the maidens made out of gold, mechanical helpers built by Hephaistos, the Greek god of metalsmiths, as described by Homer.

This was the path taken by Norbert Wiener as he opened up the cybernetic perspective, viewed as "the unified study of organisms and machines" (Wiener, 1948). One line of development linked to this approach gave rise to the familiar 'classical' human-like robot, inspired by the von Neumannian self-replicating automata and based on the top-down attitude that was typical of the "Good old-fashioned Artificial Intelligence" (Von Neumann, 1966, Harvey, 2003).

A much more interesting trend – also stemming from the seminal work of Wiener but intended to "take the human factor out of the loop" – emerged in the mid-1940s with William Grey Walter, who proposed turtle-like robots that exhibit "complex social behaviour" in responding to each other's movements and to their environment (Dorf, 1990). This was the starting point for a new behaviour-based robotics, abolishing the need for cognition as mediation between perception and plans for action.

This line of research was pursued in the 1980s by Rodney

With Henrique Garcia Pereira

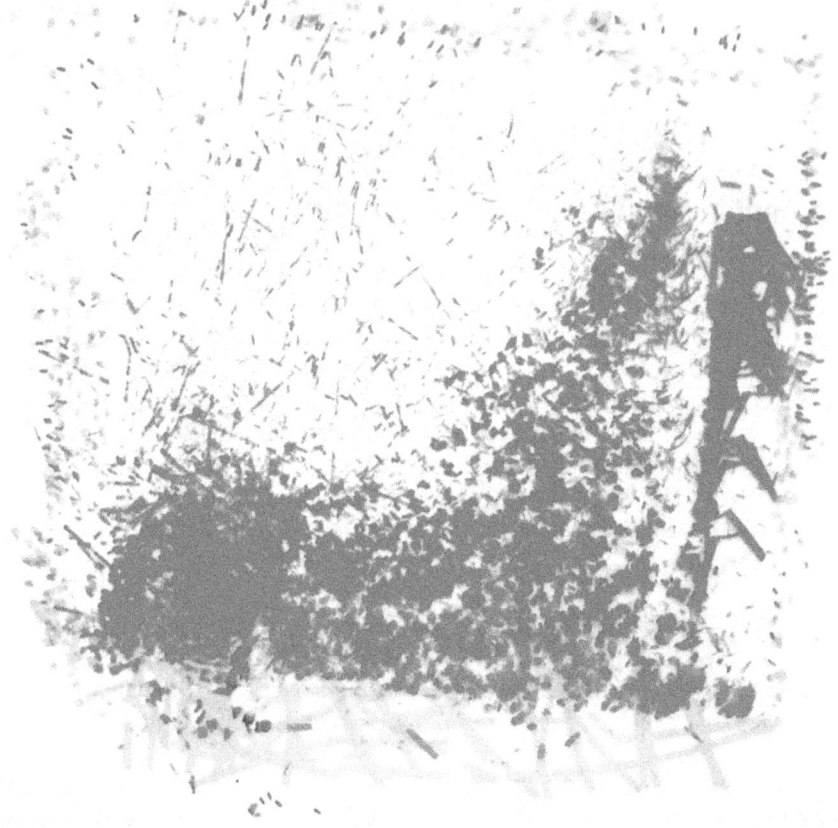

080404, 2004, acrylic on plexiglas, 100 x 100 cm

Brooks, who began building six legged "insect"-like robots at MIT.

As it was the case with 'traditional' AI robotics, where Duchamp's dictum "there is no solution because there is no problem" may find an appropriate field of application. In fact, there is no such thing as an omnipresent, instantaneous, disembodied, all-possessing eye, being able to command the robots from outside, if they have to perform complex, nonrepetitive tasks.

This 'generation' of robots was based on Brooks' novel "subsumption architecture", which describes the agent as composed of functionally distinct control levels, conceived under a layered approach that allows the addition of new layers of control without the need for changing anything in the already existing layers. The aforementioned control levels then act in the environment without supervision by a centralized control and action planning centre, as it is the case instead in traditional AI based robotics, where some kind of 'bird's eye view' always prevailed. Also, no shared representation or any low bandwidth communication system is needed. The most important concept in Brooks' reactive robots is "situatedness", which means that the robot's control mechanism refers directly to the parameters sensed in the world rather than trying to plan using an inner representation of them.

In human sciences, the concept of "situatedness" refers to the primacy of context, situation, embodieded groundness, and particular setting, favouring the bottom-up explanations that are termed "rhizomatic" in the lexicon of Deleuze and Guattari.

Linked to this concept is the "embodiment" feature, which corresponds to the fact that each "robot has a physical body and experiences the world directly through the influence of the world in that body" (Brooks, 1991). For a physically embodied robot in the real world, there are a number of key points to take into account, namely:

– Sensors deliver very uncertain values even in a stable world.

– The data delivered by sensors are not direct descriptions of the world, but rather measures of certain variables that are in fact indirect aspects of that world.

– Commands to actuators have very uncertain effects.

Basics of collective robotics

The idea of 'collective robotics' appeared in the 1990s from the convergence of the above described architecture of robots developed by Rodney Brooks with a variety of bio-inspired algorithms, focused on new programming tools for solving distributed problems. These bio-inspired algorithms stemmed from the seminal work of Christopher Langton, who launched a new avenue of research in AI denoted Artificial Life (aLife), that "allows us to break our accidental limitations to carbon-based life to explore non-biological forms of life", cf. Langton, 1987.

The well known collective behaviour of ants, bees and other eusocial insects provided the paradigm for the "swarm intelligence" approach of aLife (Bonabeau et al., 1999). This bottom-up approach is based on the assumption that systems composed of a group of simple agents can give rise to complex collective behaviour, which depends only on the interaction between those agents and the environment.

Such an interaction may occur when the environment itself is the communication medium and some form of decentralized self-organized pattern 'emerges', without being planned by any 'exterior' agency.

30   *It can be noted that this kind of behaviour corresponds to the concept of 'multitude', put forward by Hardt & Negri (2000) in antagonism to the traditional idea of 'people'. The latter shares with traditional AI some of its teleological characteristics, induced by a putative a priori 'identity'.*

The positive feedback control loop constitutes the basis for this kind of emergent morphogenesis, but randomness and fluctuations in the an individual's behaviour, far from being detrimental, may in fact greatly enhance the system's ability to explore new behaviours and find new solutions.

Collective robotics design implies an effort to keep the resources for computation, sensors and actuators as low as possible for each unit, aiming at reaching simultaneously a group behaviour as 'smart' as possible.

Industrial-military applications

The word 'robot', coined by Karel Ĉapek in his science fiction playwright R.U.R., Rossum's United Robots (1920), is derived from the Czech "robota", which refers to boring and repetitive work. Aiming at 'substituting' this type of work done by humans in factories, the first industrial robots appeared in the 1960s as huge, mechanical, hydraulically powered "arms", that soon proliferated in the production lines of automobile manufacturers. This 'industrial' goal was then conveyed to collective robotics, where a bunch of robots is charged to perform a certain task. For a variety of goals, it was shown that, ceteris paribus, a multiple-robot system composed of 'simple' agents was more effective than a single 'sophisticated' unit (an increase in the total 'utility' occurs when collective robotics is applied). For instance, in foraging, a group must pick up objects scattered in the environment. In this application, which is evocative of waste cleanup, harvest, search and rescue, collective robotics is obviously the best solution.

Given the tight intermingling between warfare and industrial R&D in the USA, it is not surprising that, prior to economics, collective robotic systems have been used for more than a decade in the military-police realm.

The image of the 'killer-robot', once belonging uniquely to the world of science-fiction, is now spread in real war scenarios as a "machine with predatory capabilities". This meets the dream of military commanders of eliminating the "human element" from the battlefield.

The Defence Advanced Research Projects Agency of the USA developed tiny reconnaissance robots acting like scouts that soldiers or commandos could carry on their backs and scatter in any 'battlefield' or space occupied by the 'enemy', in order to gather information from places where it is not possible or safe to go (Grabowsky et al., 2003).

Following the general trend for miniaturization and increase in the total number of robots, enormous networks of small agents made their appearance in January 2004, in a conference devoted to 'smart dust', the concept coined by Kristofer Pister to denote a myriad of nodes of a "Physical Internet", designed initially for detecting military devices, spread rapidly for other areas, like glacier monitoring, fire detection and environmental data capture (Larousserie, 2004). The more power structures intend to put technology at their service, the more they end up spreading it around. As Sadie Plant puts it in a somehow pompous way: "intelligence is no more on the side of power" (Plant, 1997).

Entertainement applications

Robotics has the distinction of being a branch of science to find its source in a work of fiction (Asimov's book Runaround, published in 1942). Hence, the linkage to entertainment is in the very roots of the discipline. New applications for entertainment robots, such as Sony dog robot Aibo, has sparkled companies to create a menagerie of robot toys.

As far as collective robotics is concerned, the most stunning application is probably the RoboCup Soccer, which served as test scenario for the field of multi-agent robotics (Kitano et al., 1997).

Mobile robots with navigational skills have been used in life performances in theme parks and museums (Werger, 1998) and appeared in 2002 in the theatre scene, when the MIT Media Lab introduced at the SIGGRAPH Emerging Technologies Exhibit an "Interactive Robot Theatre" (Breazeal et al., 2003). Also, the

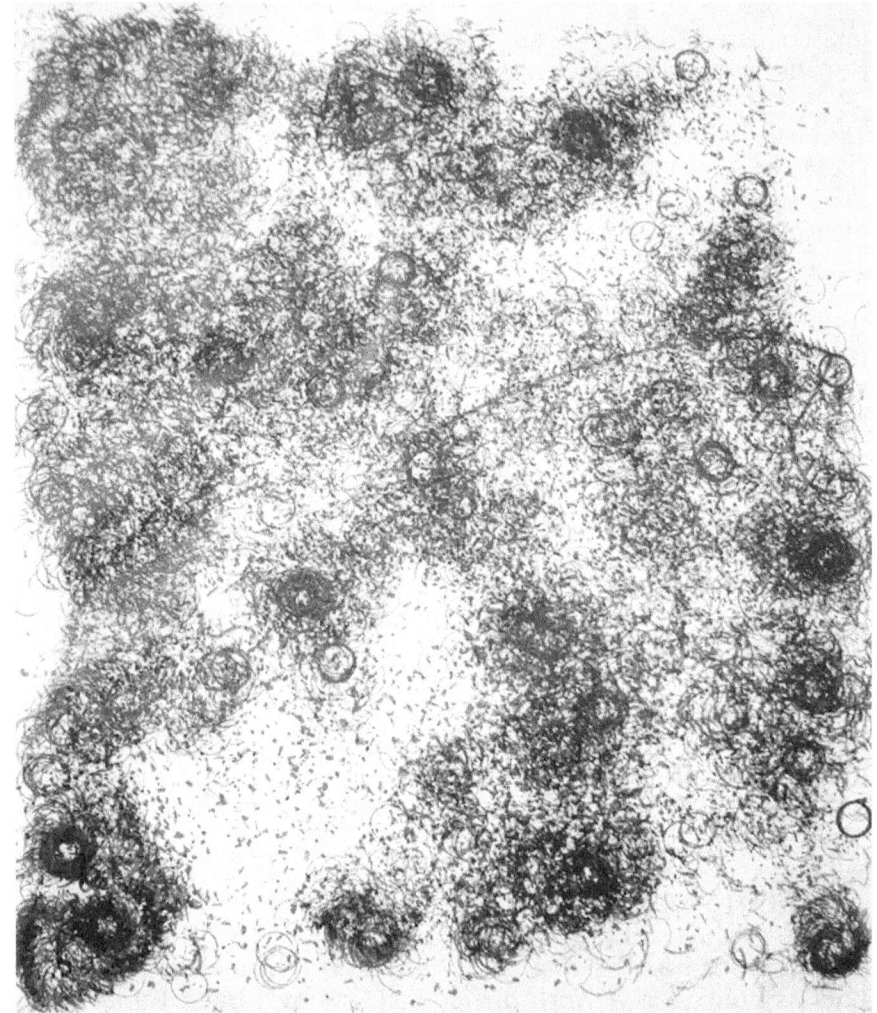

020404, 2004, acrylic on canvas, 190 x 160 cm

German pop music band "Kraftwerk" has been using a bunch of robots on stage, in order to enhance medium. In fact, this novel application of robotics may be seen as a détournement of Vivien Vienne's aphorism on architecture – "how to use space in order to waste time" (Vienne, 2000) –, by adding "and engendering dreams". In this context, where the output (art) is not accountable, 'learning' makes no sense because this feature can not be measured by any kind of 'performance index', in contrast with goal-oriented applications.

LEONEL **MOURA**

Artistic 'applications':
conceptual background of the ArtSBot project

When referring to his own masterpiece "*O livro do desas-sossego*", Fernando Pessoa stressed that its main distinctive feature was "magnificence and unusefulness" (Soares, 1998). In Pessoa's terms, no such thing as any kind of 'utility' can be ascribed to art.

This is the crucial point to be taken into account when art is produced by mechanical devices, whose goal-directed char-acteristics have obviously been of paramount importance in their former applications, both in the 'industrial-military' and entertainment domains. Hence, a profound détournement must be performed, redirecting such mechanical devices for a non-purpose of "magnificence and unusefulness".

It is obvious that any teleological setting, linked to any kind of 'objective function' (in the 'optimization' jargon), should be banned from the conceptual background behind any 'artistic' ap-plication of technology.

Simon Penny expresses this view referring to his experience as an 'Artist in Data Space': "My device is 'anti-optimised' in order to induce the maximum of 'personality'." (Penny, 1995).

The same applies, obviously, when collective robotics is though as an artistic medium. In fact, this novel application of robotics may be seen as a détournement of Vivien Vienne's aphorism on architecture – "how to use space in order to waste time" (Vienne, 2000) –, by adding "and engendering dreams". In this context, where the output (art) is not accountable, 'learning' makes no sense because this feature can not be mea-sured by any kind of 'performance index', in contrast with goal-oriented applications.

Also, the bio-inspired algorithms, with any flavour of 'fit-ness' in neo-Darwinian terms, should be carefully avoided on the grounds of Duchamp's dictum that "art has no biological source". Indeed, in contemporary societies where art assumes an ever increasing importance, there are plenty of artifacts (such as the computer, the Net, etc.) that cannot be accounted for by biological evolution. Even including the 'cultural' approach based on 'Memes', elaborated in great detail and in a variety of directions by Susan Blackmore in the sequel to the original concept introduced by Richard Dawkins as a replicator of cultural information analogous to the gene (Dawkins, 1976, Black-more, 1999)8. Memes are a blueprint for the cultural practice of 'sampling', of the 'universal copy and paste' procedure that emerged from information/communication technologies (Plant, 1997). What makes a Meme 'catchy' is not any form of 'fitness', but a fuzzy characteristic denoted by mètis in the ancient Greek thought (a kind of sagesse combining sagacity and 'flair', attention and malleability, prevision and simulation, opportunity and practical skills).

The dual mind/body problem (that has been floating over Western thought since Descartes) is to be overcome by the 'horizontal' synergetic combination of both components, discarding any type of hierarchy, in particular the Cartesian value system, which privileges the abstract and disembodied over the concrete and embodied.

The approach proposed here follows tightly the interconnectedness of being and its formal embodiment as inseparable parts of autopoiesis, in Maturana & Varela's sense. In visual arts, a similar point is made by Sean Cubitt, when he claims that contemporary artworks must construct their own local, not presume it. In Cubbitt's words: "the digital art must be material". This is the paradox that drives all new approaches on the production of 'concrete' artworks by using information technologies.

Along these lines, when conceiving his robots, Rodney Brooks argues that natural beings are not products only of their genes, but of their interaction with environment, which can be simulated in robots by a stimulus-response system. Hence, elaborate behaviour in robots is elicited by wiring sensors directly to actuators, under the above mentioned approach, based on "situatedness" and "embodiment".

From Langton's aLife paradigm, the point to be stressed here is 'life as it could be' and not as it is: no swarm of 'social insects' is needed to inspire artistic oriented robots, since the artist, by contrast with insects. is absolutely work adverse.

The building capacity of termites, the cooperative foraging strategies such as trail recruitment and corpse-gathering in ants are features contradictory with artistic non-purposes.

The idea of process-based or generative art may be grounded on some important aLife's rules, under the condition that those rules allow for the autonomous operation of an artifact employed as an artistic device. Indeed, when creators do want to loose control over their creations, what counts is a local interaction of components giving rise to a global outcome which is not explicitly coded in the components, i.e., a whole that is "greater than the sum of its parts". This is the case that may be made when applying aLife to purposeless unmanned art, where morphic resonance is the key point, adjusted to Derrida's attitude vis-à-vis the basic element of inscription, the graphic trace, or grapheme, as he terms it.

Morphic resonance is a concept put forward by Rupert Sheldrake, aiming to ex- *plain why, once an artificial life form comes into being in a given configuration, it is more likely that the same configuration will occur in the future (Sheldrake, 1981)*

This element imposes its own constraints on the production of meaning, which is not moulded to the demands of either pre-given objectives or already constituted meaning (Derrida, 1967). In urban theory, a city may be seen as a set of "traces", assembled in space by successive "gestures" (cf. Lefebvre, 1968).

To the best of our knowledge, ArtSBot is the first experiment where collective robotics is applied in the artistic realm.

The project produces artworks by means of the interaction, through the environment, of a group of robots carrying two marking-pens as a painting device. The basics of the algorithm uploaded to each robot's microcontroller through a PC serial interface consists of a positive feedback mechanism that leads to the reinforcement, by a current robot, of the colours left in the canvas by a previous passage of another robot. The process is initialized by a random procedure and it is stopped by the human feeling that the artwork is 'complete'.

In fact, the way robots evolve in the initial steps of their routes evokes irresistibly the surrealist's dérive, a haphazard deambulation in a city. Then, as long as interaction increases, the dérive come to terms with its détournement, as carried out by the Situationist International in the 1950s.

Situationists criticized surrealist deambulation on the grounds of the exaggerated importance assigned to the unconscious and to chance. In Debord's words, the dérive "in its infancy would be partly dependent upon chance and would have to accommodate a degree of letting go".

The situationist's dérive is a collective art form, an aesthetic operation that had the power to annul the individual components of the artwork, since it is performed in group. By this token, the urban space is an "objective passional terrain" rather

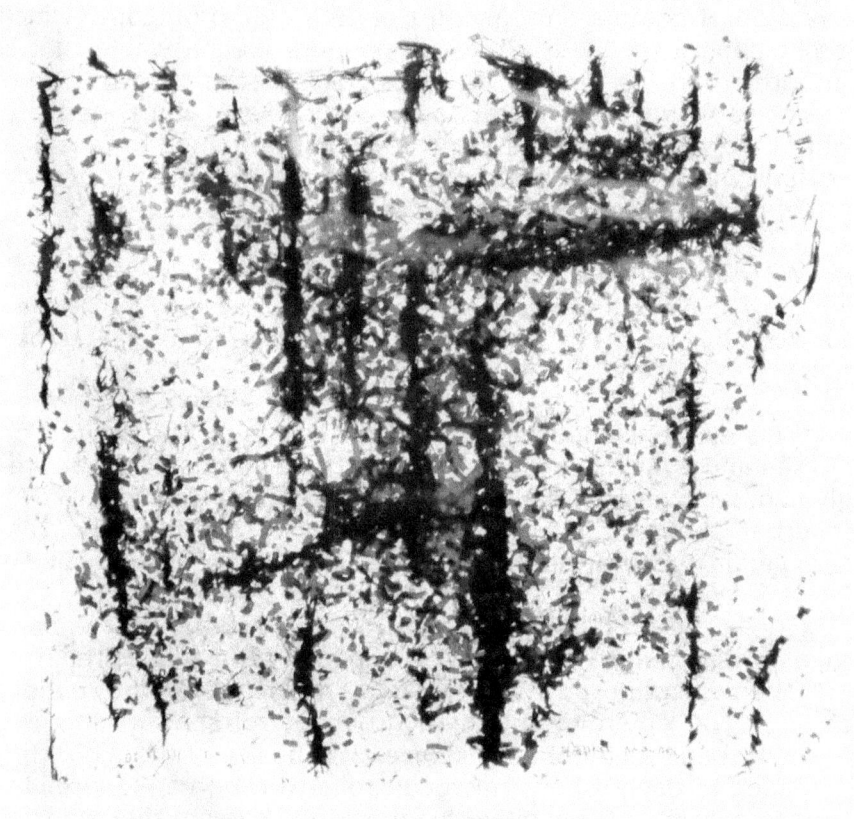

020604, 2004, acrylic on canvas, 120 x 120 cm

than merely subjective-unconscious. The dérive was, in fact, an action hard to fit into the art system, as it consisted in constructing the modes of a "situation" that leaves no sign. But it agrees perfectly with Dada logic of anti-art.

The positive feedback mechanism may be seen as the driving force for revisiting certain spots of the city, which were considered particularly appealing in former passages. This corresponds to a psycogeographical study of urban space, with its currents, fixed points and vortexes, which bring to mind the dynamics of chaotic systems. The identification of emotionally interesting places within space will (over time) reinforce the distinction that put them in a privileged situation for the group participating in the dérive experiment. This leads to an 'emogram', a map of emotive impressions, which is the analogue, in urban situationist terms, of the final artwork performed by the group of robots.

But, at any instance, there is always place for the unexpected, since the random factor coexists with the above mentioned accumulative configuration, along the entire process.

In contemporary terms, the situationist's dérive is pursued by several groups. The Italian Stalker group considers walking as a critical tool, and as a form of emergence of a certain kind of art that develops architecture of "situated objects". This group's attitude is inspired by the Italian expression "andare a Zonzo", which means to waste time wandering aimlessly. The fractal character of contemporary cities is recognized by Francesco Careri, when experiencing a series of "interruptions and reprises, fragments of the constructed city and unbuilt zones that alternate in a continuous passage from full to empty and back" (Careri, 2003).

Another way of looking at the ArtSBot experiment is inspired by the surealist *cadavre exquis*.

The first experience of this type was performed in 1925 by Duhamel, Prévert and Tanguy in literary terms. The first sentence that emerged was "Le cadaver exquis boira le vin nouveau".

This 'game' involved a group of persons that contributed to a collective artwork of which they only knew, until the final outcome, their individual part. When one of the players finishes his 'work', the sheet of paper upon which he had drawn is folded in order to hide his contribution, except in a small part, which is the starting point for the next player.

Similarly, in our experiment, each robot does not have the 'general picture'; he 'must' rely on the clue left by a previous passage of another robot.

Giving up definitively of the anthropocentric prejudice that underlies the creation of human-like robots, the points that are retained here from the aLife attitude are stigmergy (in Grassé's terms), decentralization, autonomy, self-organization, emergence and interaction between agents via the environment.

Since Foucault's announcement of the "death of the subject" in the 1970s, a decentred self emerged, driven by the digital revolution. One has to make one's own history in terms of how it would be traversed by the question of the relationship between structures of rationality and procedures of subjugation which are linked to it. Hence, it becomes more and more difficult for each person to remain absolutely in agreement with oneself (identity is defined by trajectories). Also, now in Derrida's terms, this deconstructed subject is a person with no fixed identity, with no fixed principles, and without any base for ethics. But

Duchamp had already made the same case, when he answered to Cabanne's question – "What do you believe in?" – by an abrupt: "Nothing, of course". And he added that he did not believe in the word 'being', since he viewed it as "a human invention". In regard to the issue of his own identity drift, he said by 1963 that the notion of anti-art annoyed him because "whether you are anti- or for-, it's two sides of the same thing" (Cameron, 1992). Moreover, he had momentarily 'changed his identity' in 1921, when – as a pioneer of what is nowadays currently performed in the Net – he asked Man Ray to photograph him as a woman named "Rrose Sélavy". Also, his famous "Fountain" was sent to the 1917 exhibition of the American Society of Independent Artists by someone called R. Mutt. In fact, Duchamp wrote to his sister:" One of my female friends, under a masculine pseudonym, Richard Mutt, sent in a porcelain urinal as a sculpture" (Duve, 1992).

Also, the case of 'imitation' is to be addressed here, leading to complexity via the 'explosive' accumulation and recombination of simple unitary actions. The importance of 'imitation' in human societies was raised by the often neglected French sociologist Gabriel Tarde. In Tarde's approach, what is meant by 'culture' stems from the reinforcement of a given stimulus, caused by the imitation of a certain behaviour or idea. Tarde's approach, transposed in contemporary terms as positive feedback, is in the roots of Dawkins' 'meme' concept.

Some kind of positive feedback, coupled with a hint of randomness, is the driving force behind the attitude of the group of painter-robots, which produces novelty by unexpected change in the spatial arrangement of traces in the canvas.

The roots of randomness in art may be found in the technique behind a pictorial practice that appeared in 'minor' circles of the Italian 16th century mannerism – the "pittura a capriccio". This technique consisted of applying on the canvas, without referent, quick and successive ink spots, "picked up directly from the artist's mind". All the 'automatic' surrealistic approach stems from this basic attitude, by adding sometimes a light psychoanalysis flavour. In the 1970s, Wols used to say that when he begins to paint, he does not know what he is going to paint. This turns out to be a veritable methodology, as noted by Fréchuret, 2001, when he writes: "Ne pas savoir ce que le pinceau, la brosse ou le racloir va laisser comme traces devient très précisémment l'enjeu d'une technique qui, à l'aveuglette, se constitue peu à peu".

Since no pre-defined plan commands the global behaviour of the group of robots, this experiment can be interpreted at the light of Lefebvre's idea that "Topos is prior to logos" (Lefebvre, 1968).

Aesthetic creation is defined here as a set of transformative rules that claims for a vital examination of all stages of the aesthetic production/consumption process, instead of overrating the output (as it used to come about when art was considered as a 'matter of taste').

The case to be made here has nothing to do with 'evolutionary robotics'. Whilst, in this theoretical topic the aim is to address hard questions about how life may occur, in the practical realm of the ArtSBot project the aim is to experience ephemeral situations leading to novelty and surprise, where art may occur. Here, no evolutionary perspective is needed and no rank order is admissible.

In contemporary societies where the artificial prevails, there is no point in replicating the ancient drive of our ancestors to locate food, mate and protect off-springs.

Using the concept of 'network semiotics', Joel Slayton has demonstrated that complex systems exhibiting an autocatalytic pattern do not show any adaptive tendency towards optimisation of resources or 'efficiency'. Rather, there is a continuous shifting among possible phase alternatives. The network semiotic moves between different states of equilibrium in a response to the multitude of uncertain objectives represented as expressions of network applications (Slayton, 1998). Hence, "the purpose for action", put by Max Weber in the core of "power", is being dismissed (or at least dispersed) in post-Fordian societies where complexity prevails (i.e., when we move from the Guttenberg galaxy to the Internet galaxy, in Castell's terms).

In particular, in what concerns the old predator/prey problem, it should be noted that if life forms usually act in a predatory manner, conversely, "only living forms would have need not to" (Shanken, 2001). Also, Foucault's critique of what he names "biopolitics" – as a mode of organizing and regulating a population considered as biological species in the sense of normalizing large scale groupings of "docile bodies" – should be taken into account when analogies based on "life as it is" are performed.

Cultural hybridization of science and art

Historical perspective

Despite their apparent opposition, science and art were always closely intermingled, since they draw their common groundwork from the dominant cultural context of each epoch.

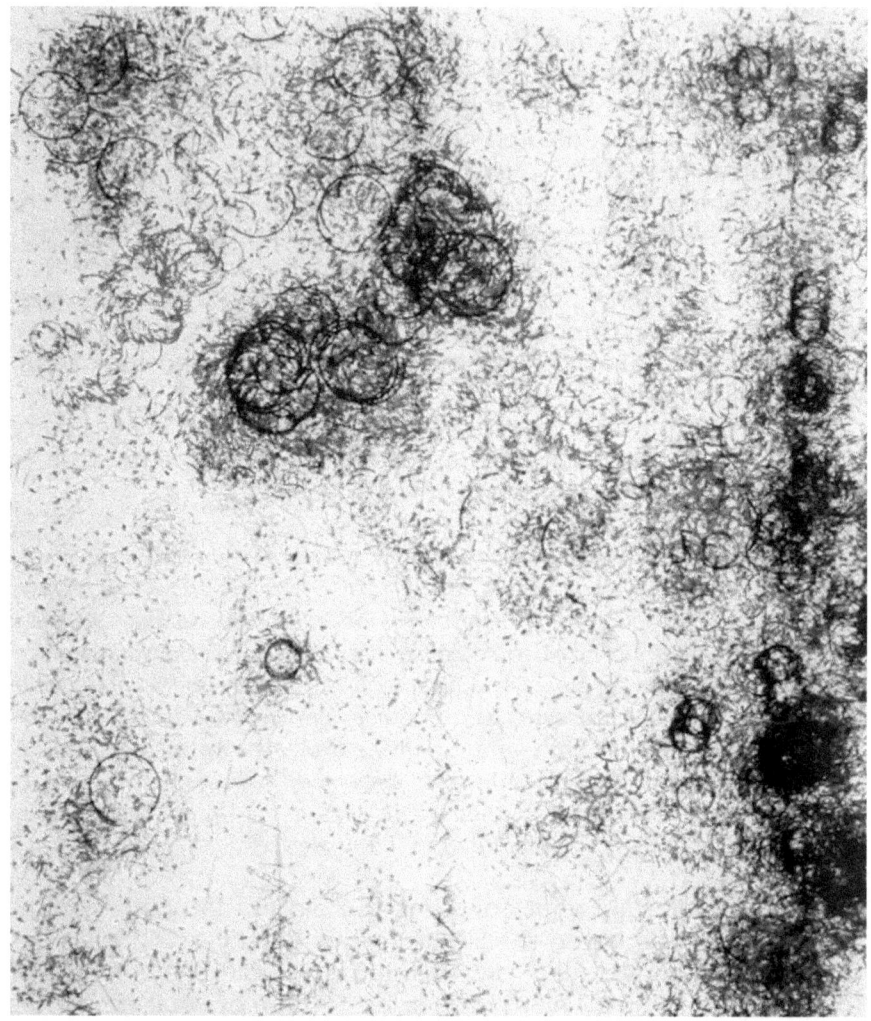

150304, 2004, acrylic on canvas, 190 x 160 cm

This opposition was constructed under the pressure of the Hellenic ideological divide, whose repercussion goes far beyond its remote foundation. In fact, the 'Greek' line of thought put science in an elevated 'philosophical' domain, while art was disqualified in the 'worthless' realm of the techné.

In the 16th century Renaissance, both activities reached a peak of cross-fertilization, under the influence of Leonardo's striking polyvalence. In particular, the multi-talented painter-engineer drew plans for a mechanical man. Moreover, Leonardo

LEONEL **MOURA**

da Vinci understands the interest of Aristotle's Camera Obscura for artistic purposes, projecting 'Nature' onto an artificial plan, which is the basis for representation. Along the same lines, Francesco Algarotti claims, in the 18th century, that painters should make use of the Camera Obscura as scientists apply the microscope or the telescope to grasp "the rules of Nature". And even when the 'Enlightenment' brought the importance of science to its ideological 'climax', a certain kind of convergence with art is noticeable, by contrast with commonsensical beliefs.
During this period of intense cultural effervescence, scientists searched in matter the signs of 'the Works of God', whilst artists, influenced by the sentiments of Romanticism, saw their role as 'Divine Messengers'. For these apparently opposed ideologies – positivism vs. romanticism -, the goal was the same, only the modus faciendi - empirical vs. phenomenological - was different.

When Paul Cézanne, considered by the mainstream as "the father of modern art", uttered his celebrated dictum that forms in painting should be reduced to basic geometrical elements, he initiated, through his artistic praxis, an important development that led to Cubism. This was designated in Penny, 1995, as the 'industrialization of vision'.

It is worth noting that this approach ultimately found realization in 3D computer graphics almost a century later. Also, as remarked by Plant, 1997, artificial life pursues the very same goals that Paul Cézanne proposed when he said: "Art is harmony parallel to nature". In this sense, aLife researchers are artists in Cézanne's terms, since their goal is not to represent the world, but to 'render visible'.

Going further in reducing the basic elements of painting to points, the 'pointillist' attitude disclosed some features of Wolfgang Köler's "Gestalt Psycologismus", that came to light in 1929 (Köler, 2000) in the sequel of Wertheimer's work. In fact, a pointillist tableau makes no sense, except if it is globally conceived (and perceived).

There is also an analogy with this issue in music. To grasp the meaning of a choral piece, it is not enough to listen to the individual singers one-by-one: the performers should be listen to as a 'whole', given that they modulate their voices and timing in response to one another. In general terms, the neuronal activity of 'perception' implies always a combination of sensory systems to form a gestalt (Freeman, 1991).

When photographic reproduction appeared by the mid of the 19th century, a complete rupture in regard to naturalism occurs naturally: there is no point to imitate nature, since the same role is performed by photography in a much more reliable way. This obviously opens the way to abstractionism.

In regard to the avant-garde movements prevailing in the artistic scene until the middle of the 20th century, they seem in general to be characterized by a deeply ambivalent relationship with science, which became increasingly implicated in wars and capitalistic-bureaucratic ideologies.

Hence, the liberating 'flavour' of science almost eclipses, under the repulsion caused by its dreadful consequences. But, paradoxical as it may seem, Dada, the most radical libertarian artistic anti-war movement that bitterly accused 'science' of being behind the 1914-18 genocide, included among its most influential 'members' Marcel Duchamp, an engineer fascinated by physics, non-Euclidean geometries and chess, and his friend Francis Picabia, who praised velocity and the automobile as signs of 'modern times', characterized in first place by the Industrial Revolution scientific discoveries. Duchamp's ready-mades included, for instance a bicycle wheel, which can be viewed as a scientific commentary on movement and stability. Also Picabia's machinist style is apparent in many of his works.

There is nothing inherent in any creation that makes it out 'art'. Duchamp's ready-mades are mass product objects, selected by the artist and elevated to the realm of 'art' by virtue of having been chosen (in Duchamp words: "They are a kind of rendez-vous"). The ready-made producer underscores the 'object' itself, as well as its manufacturing process, emphasising rather the context where the object is situated. Whilst a 'classic artwork' is yet 'art' even when withdrawn from the 'museum', a ready-made by itself is no more than trash – its 'merit' stems from the context (the place where it is put on display).

Surrealists (in some instances) brought intensive randomness to the realm of art. This feature can be considered as a constructive apport, when no psychoanalyst flavour is added. In fact, putting the umbrella and the typewriter on the space of the operating table works because the viewer recognizes the juxtaposition of the improbable. This can be linked to the contingent character of contemporary scientific models, namely in biology, where chance plays a crucial role, if evolution is seen as a consequence of improbable mutations (in the line of Jacob, Monot, Gould).

The cultural 'heirs' of Dada radical attitude in the artistic revolutionary scene of the 1950s and 1960s – Lettrists and Situationists – maintained the aforementioned ambivalent attitude towards science. By contrast with Debord's criticism of the "re-cuperative" capabilities of capitalism in the merchandise realm, another line of though – represented by Asger Jorn, Giuseppe Pinot-Gallizio and, above all, by Constant Nieuwenhuys – was enthusiastic in what concerns the egalitarian content of a wide range of scientific disciplines, mainly mechanics, automation and cybernetics.

In parallel with pointillism, the Lettrists made a case on the role of the 'letter' 43
as the basic element of writing. If early Lettrist activity was centred on sound poetry, the emphasis soon shifted to visual art production, maintaining how-ever the 'letter' as the basic subject of aesthetic contemplation. One important contribution to contemporary though made by Isou, an early Lettrist, was the central role that he attributed (since 1948!) to young culture. Also, Debord's initial writings of the Lettrist phase emphasise the "removal of substance" – an-other important topic in contemporary thought –, by "extracting the letter from the voice and setting it free".
The radical theorists of the Situationist International (IS), relying upon the cre-ation of emotionally appealing 'situations', have pursued the Lettrist theoreti-cal effort, putting forward by the middle of the 20th century some important concepts, like dérive, psycogeography and détournement. This attitude was far ahead of its time, except for brief but intense revolutionary flashes. Nonsurpris-ingly, some of the concepts developed decades ago by the situationists are now in the core of a persistent line of though underlying an egalitarian view of the information/communication technologies. In fact, when the 'new media' are scrutinized by social sciences, a number of collaborative attitudes are spotted, for example in the so-called 'hackers', as opposed to the hierarchical structure of the old media. This collaborative strategy, characterized by self-organization, solidarity and gift finds some of its roots in the IS philosophy. Moreover, it can be noted that what Debord called détounement in 1956 – "any elements, no matter where they are taken from, can serve in making new combinations" – is, on a greater scale, the system by which most human technology develop. Innovations are generally a very minor discovery, resulting from a synthesis of the already known.

In this view, science was prone to liberate man from forced work, 'leaving space' to the development of prodigality, collab-orative strategies, solidarity and, above all, to the emergence of a 'gift culture' based on 'energy wasting', as an alternative to the 'energy conservation' that was characteristic of the In-dustrial Revolution. In Georges Bataille's approach, the surplus that contemporary society has at its disposal is to be "applied in games and spectacles that derive therefrom, or personal luxu-ry" (Bataille, 1967).

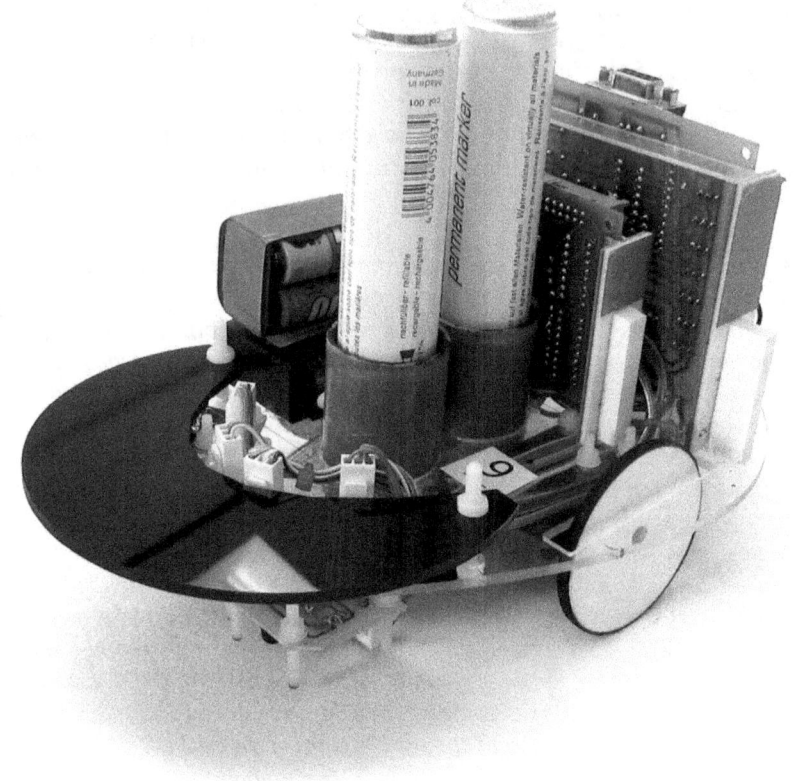

Ant-like painting robot, 2003

This cultural shift was announced by the influential Dutch scholar Johan Huizinga in his 1938 classic «Homo Ludens», which is an obvious source in situationist literature, as well as Marcel Mauss' anthropologic study of the "potlatch" among Northwest American Indians, which corresponds to a redistribution of goods in fierce competitions of generosity. In fact, situationists claim for a society of pleasure instead of the stoicism and sacrifice of Stalinism or the peer pressure of consumerism. In this regard, situationists pioneered contemporary awareness of the importance of leisure, instead of labour, as a revolutionary weapon. Therefore, both Guy Debord and Asger Jorn criticized acutely le Corbusier's "machine à habiter" and Bauhaus functionalism, condemning their underlying monstrous ideology of a 'homogeneous' and 'massive' urbanism that opens the doors

to procedures of containment, exclusion, surveillance and individual control. These procedures tend to destroy the 'living'
parts of the city, those indigenous working-class zones disclosed
by psycogeographic studies. As an example of the outcome of
such a studies, they exhibited the map of Paris obtained through
the "clustering" of the city. Each cluster corresponds to an "uni-
té d'ambiance", a locus where the 'soft' mutable elements of
the city scene coexist with the 'hard' architectural structures on
which the former are grounded. But, in stark contrast with the
idea of a full refusal of any type of art proposed by Debord, Asger
Jorn believed in the collective, and noncompetitive production of
art, viewed obviously not as a high culture product of capitalistic
societies, but as a process giving rise to 'cultural artifacts' that
are to disappear from museums only to reappear everywhere.

Another development emanated from surrealist automatism can be found in Pollock's drip paint technique. Applied onto
enormous sheets of canvas spread on the floor, it called the
attention of mathematicians that analysed it in terms of the
experimental patterns produced. The conclusion reached was
that those patterns followed Mandelbrot's fractal models, i.e.
shapes found in Nature that repeats themselves on different
scales within the same object (cf. Taylor et. al., 1999). In Pollock's work hermeneutics, complexity may also be invoked when
vortices of concentration of ink spots, roughly 'clusters', arise.
Those may be interpreted as the effect of strange attractors, as
considered by non-linear dynamic systems theory.

The rapid diffusion of systems theory in the 1960s gave rise
to a new 'aesthetical' attitude, which "puts cybernetics as the
theoretical ground for contemporary art" (Penny, 1999). On the
other hand, science is now completely immersed in the framework of cultural production, in parallel with its rich tradition of
detailed micro-studies directed at experiments, instruments
and processes.

Impact of the digital revolution on creativity

Nowadays, the Zeitgeist is dominated by the digital revolution. Simon Penny summarized this piece of evidence through
this witty contemporary truism: "The list of things to do before
locking up the house includes putting out the cat, turning off the
oven and backing up the hard drive". (Penny, 1995). The same
author makes the point that, surprisingly, such an ubiquitous
device as the computer was developed without any influence of
the most influential thinkers of the 20th century! This 'strange'

fact can be grasped if one cogitates on the impossibility of accounting for any kind of bifurcation by classical Western philosophy based on linear 'progress'.

The Net, which may be considered the most important technological breakthrough since the Guttenberg Revolution, was not 'predicted' by any prior 'science fiction' authors, who were bounded by linear extrapolations of the achievements of their Zeitgeist.

New forms of creativity, both in science and art, are conveyed by the 'dematerialization' brought to light by an intensive use of information/communication technologies, which have an immense amplifying power.

The term 'dematerialisation' was coined by American critics John Chandler and Lucy Lippard to describe an important characteristic of the artistic movements prevailing in the 1960s. This term, referring loosely to the physical disintegration of the traditional 'matter' of art and representing an aesthetic attack on the primacy of painting and sculpture, symbolizes a radical gesture directed against an increasingly overbearing art market, not against 'material' in itself. (Chandler & Lippard, 1968)

Hence, instead of pursuing their former 'reductionist' interpretation of Nature (based on some 'solvable' differential equations systems), scientists are increasingly involved in, and concerned with, complex epistemological questions stemming from the new disciplines of the artificial, namely the Turing Test and John Searle's Chinese Room Argument, and addressing the problem of establishing the criteria for judging if "Machines can think". Obviously, along these lines, limits in space and time are abolished.

The Turing test for intelligent machines consists of putting behind a curtain an human and behind another curtain a computer; if, after five minutes, an interrogator has no better than a 50% chance of distinguishing human and computer, the computer is intelligent. Searle's Chinese Room consists of considering a computer program for understanding (written) Chinese; carrying only a book containing the instructions of such a program, John Searle goes inside a closed room which has an input and an output slot; whenever a squiggle comes in, Searle looks in the book for what to do and provides an output; even though this room has exactly (over time!) the same (written) language behaviour as a native Chinese, there is no 'understanding' going out there.

It is worth noting, however, that most dematerialization supporters – who are, in general, 'genuine' materialists adverse to the rhetoric of 'transcendence via the Net' – do not intend to get out of matter, but they want to get out of the confining organization of matter which is ideologically shaped into things and organisms by the ancient conservative and traditionalist powers. Here, Derrida's concern on the materiality of the signifier – challenging the usual disembodied Platonist mathematics – is met on its implications for construction meaning as an endless process of textual difference.

Nowadays, it can be stated that the arrival of the Net sig-nalled the recommencement of an emancipatory project based on creativity, communication and a 'gift economy'. A symptom of this new trend, based on the fact that 'information' escapes from any zero-sum game, comes from the failure to use Internet exclusively for commercial ends. Also, the appearance and expansion of public domain and open source software like Linux is another sign of the possibility of escaping from the empire of commodity that was supposed to rule utterly human behaviour.

Sean Cubbit, in an interview given on January 2003, considers Linux as one of the finest artworks of the 20th century. Also, he puts the case that, whenever one is online, this means that s/he is functioning at the margin (Trace, Online writing Centre).

As the process of digital convergence accelerates, divisions between different professions are being broken down and C. P. Snow's divide between the "Two cultures" is getting somehow thinner.

The conceptual fluidity that allows nomad ideas to migrate from one field to another is enormously facilitated by the common zero+ones basis where everything relies on. In fact, the more abstract the concept (and electronic media are the apex of abstraction), the greater the number of other concepts that are potentially evoked by it.

This feature was extensively exploited by Jean-François Lyothard, the celebrated author of the nowadays classic 1979 book "The Postmodern Condition", who put into practice his idea of 'drift' from one direction to another (and from a subject to another) as Curator of the exhibition "les immateriaux", held in 1985 at the Centre Beaubourg in Paris. In this exhibition science was mixed with art in a variety of ways, under a common digital underlying environment.

In contemporary art, the "code" is the structuring system of the artwork, putting across the paradoxical meaning of a text, which is also a (virtual) machine. The digital technologies give

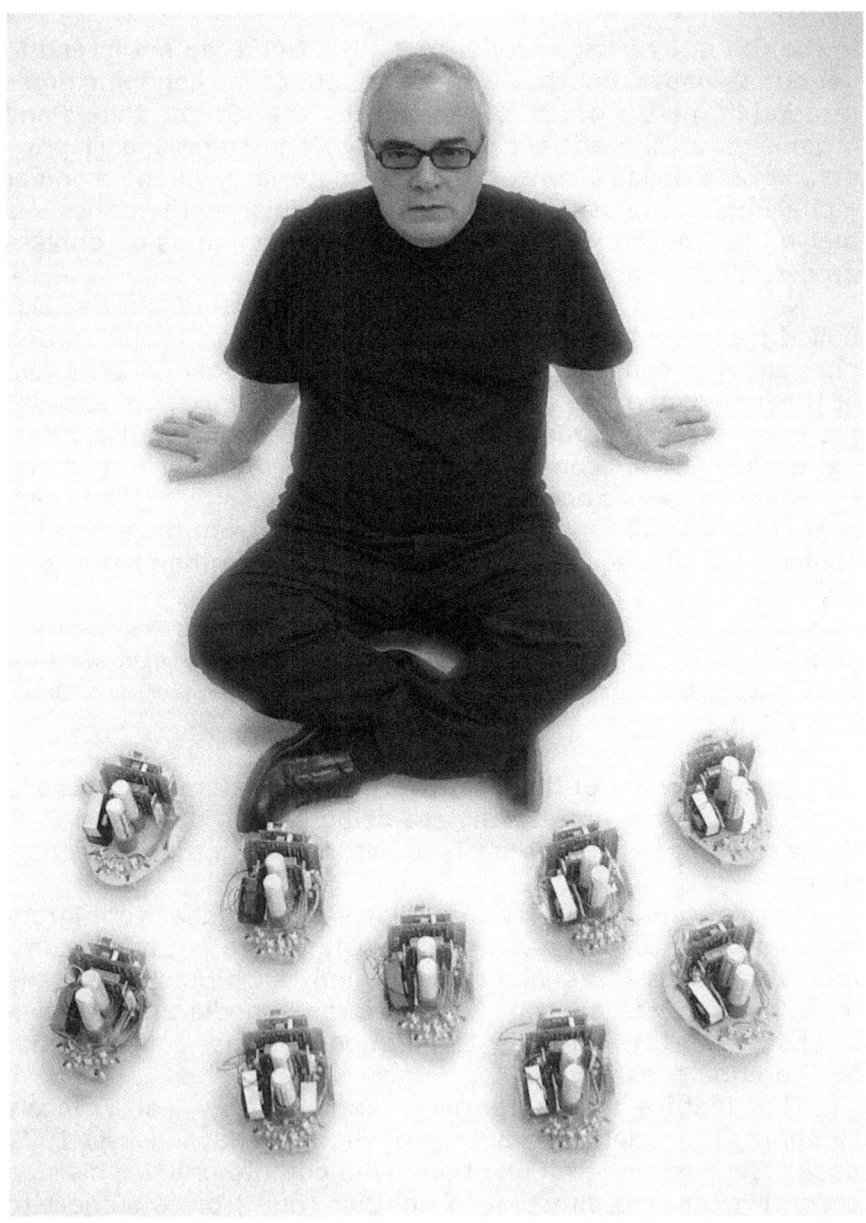

With swarm of painting robots

rise to a malleable aesthetics, based on the principle that anything that can be made can be remade.

On the other hand, the sciences of complexity, conveying

their concepts of bifurcation, deterministic chaos and strange attractors, brought a new insight to the analysis of creativity, inasmuch as it is no more plausible to see invention stemming from any essentialist kind of 'genius'.

In Herbert Simon words: "Chaos derives from deterministic dynamic systems that, if their initial conditions are disturbed may alter their paths radically. Although they are deterministic, their detailed behaviour over time is unpredictable, for small perturbations cause large changes in path." (Simon, 1997).
Deleuze & Guattari, 1980, introduced the concept of "machinephylum" to refer to the overall set of self-organizing processes in the universe. This notion allows the establishing of connections between information/communication technologies and auto-catalystic processes. In fact, the singularities at the onset of those processes are critical points in the flow of matter and energy that can be represented by the same models that are in the core of "abstract machines".

Contemporary views on this topic privileges 'inversion' over 'inspiration'. This means that any creative breakthrough is not 'random', but is based on the scrutiny of prior canons and codes, followed by a bifurcation driven by a strange attractor, whose 'basin of attraction' prevails over the former mainstream tendency.

The creativity issue was also approached at the MIT on the grounds of complexity science (Slayton, 1998). The experiments conducted since the 1980s in the context of emergent conversation (a sort of computer-based 'brainstorming') lead to the (provisional) conclusion that, since there is no specific objective or purposes guiding the conversational system, a continuous shifting among possible phase alternatives occurs.

This was interpreted by autocatalytic patterns, which are signified only by the computational structure of data. Also it was clearly remarked that the meshwork grows in "unplanned" directions, evidencing the tendency of subsystems for adaptation towards less than optimum goals. In this context, since there is no such thing as any 'objective function' (in the optimization jargon), it is virtually impossible to determine non-subjectively the relative merits of the diverse combinations.

Moreover, the digital revolution bridged the sharp divide that used to occur between two distinct types of knowledge: knowledge-how (colloquially denoted by know-how) and 'knowledge-whether', the ability that the physicist Mike Greenhough has identified as the recognition of something being 'just right'.

This newcomer concept in the 'hard' disciplines where quantification used to be the nec plus ultra (Rutherford believed that "qualitative is nothing but poor quantitative") goes along with Bachelard's 'approximate knowledge' that is embedding all branches of science from Heisenberg to Zadeh.

In this context, Keynes summarized the new attitude in science trough the acute statement : "It's better to be roughly right than precisely wrong".

In fact, the knowledge-whether model had been clearly formulated in 1950 by E. H. Gombrich in his classic "The story of art". The example given by Gombrich to explain the 'sense of rightness' refers to a nonexpert arranging a bunch of flowers. At a certain point, which would correspond loosely to the 'optimum' (in Operations Research jargon), the process stops because 'it is felt' that another step (any act of adding, removing, substituting, merging or relocating a flower) would jeopardize the outcome. Such a point of 'homogenized diversity' can be interpreted in connectionist terms as the solution of a 'constraint satisfaction' problem, where a stabilizing factor induces the satisfaction of a maximum number of constraints, via an extended interaction with our environment and all cultural and social values it embodies (Page, 2000). Therefore, artists and scientists are nowadays indistinguishable in their attempts to measure, translate, transpose and generally deal with the shock of the 'new'.

'Robotic Art': critique of interactivity

The pioneer work of Simon Penny in 'robotic art' was developed since 1989, when the current Director of ACE (Arts Computing Engineering Graduate Program) of the University of California produced Petit Mal, an autonomous robot artwork that "reacted to people". Even though avoiding anthropomorphism, zoomorphism and biomorphism, the goal of "interaction with humans" made this experience seriously vulnerable, since it is virtually impracticable at the current stage of technology to reduce human behaviour to algorithmic functions and to represent the response of the system back to the user. Simon Penny's attitude, however, was important in his critical assessment of the rhetoric surrounding VR, on the grounds of its ultimately antimaterialistic and anti-embodying qualities, metaphorised as dreams of transcendence and delivery from the prison of flesh (Penny et. al., 2000).

On the other end, the line of thought where Penny is situated stresses the importance of the 'interaction with the public' through the promotion of 'transactional happenings', where it supposedly occur some collaboration of the receiver. But, despite the last 40 years myriad of 'happenings', the disturbing impression arises that nothing is happening in interactive art – an era of hypothermia of artistic interaction with the 'public' seems to be overrunning the cultural arena of the last decades.

Since the emerging of multimedia performance art in New York in the 1960s that the situationists denounced their 'spectacular' character that leaves the 'spectacle' unchanged, without leading to any kind of transformation of consciousness among their 'participants'. The 1963 volume 8 of "Internationale Situationniste" writes: "happenings are a hash produced by throwing together all the artists leftovers".

This impression may derive from the novel fact that the obligatory link between art and dissent disappeared since the disappearance of the 20th century avant-garde movements, in which such a link was taken for granted.

Permeability between contemporary art, politics and philosophy

Art in the context of massive technocapitalism

Walter Benjamin, in his decisive 1931 essay on "The Work of Art in the Age of Mechanical Reproduction" (Benjamin, 1978), anticipates a constellation of characteristics that apply to contemporary 'works of art', altering the classic western aesthetic conception established during the Renaissance:
1. The demise of the halo of originality
2. A coexistence of many copies of the same image
3. An undermining of the concept of the artist as a 'genius'
4. New challenges stimulated through the independence of the art work from originality
5. Democratization of the art market place
6. Contemporary possibilities for new social meanings of art

In the sequel of the central argument of Benjamin, referring to the erosion of the uniqueness and singularity of the work of art, questions of authenticity and origin – which fundamentally grounded the aesthetic experience of modernist contemplation – became completely displaced.

In fact, Dada announced Barthes's "death of author" when a group of individuals - Hausman, Grosz, Baader, Herzfeld -

'signed' his artworks under the multiple name of "Christ & Co. Ltd." This concept of multiple authorship under a common 'label' reappeared in 1994, in Italy, where a set of writers founded some kind of a 'literary factory' denoted by the collective name of 'Luther Blissett' and aimed at "building narratives". Along the same lines, a ' private firm' providing 'narrative services' in a variety of media was launched in Bologna in 1999.

This 'firm', labelled 'Wu Ming' (a Chinese 'logo' that means "no name"), is a 'lab of literary design' that puts emphasis on 'brainwork', the most important post-fordist 'production factor'. Furthermore, Wu Ming does not avoid 'spectacular' publicity, as it was the case with previous avant-garde groups, namely the IS, that considered any concrete democratic acquis or any popular culture achievement as prone to be "recuperated" by capitalism, strengthening by this means the 'spectacle society', as coined by Debord.

In regard to another IS concern – the end of copyright –, contemporary dissent movements linked to the fight against neo-liberal globalisation agree completely with the situationist attitude, enlarging it to every existing communication medium, like the Internet. But the practice of sampling the work of others is hardly new. For centuries, artists have plagiarised their predecessor and contemporaries, since all collective endeavours involve a constant process of re-processing (Lautréamont is a notorious plagiarism supporter). If intellectual property had existed in ancient times – in fact it stems from the Enlightenment individualism – , humanity would not be acquainted with Mahabharata, Sun Tzu, The Odyssey or The Arabian Nights. The information/communication technologies have make the 'sampling' practice much easier and more aesthetically pleasing, suppressing by peer-to-peer networks the distinction between original' and 'copy'.

This had very deep consequences in contemporary art, since aesthetic experience can no longer be isolated from the social conditions which have made its production, dissemination and reception possible.

The aforementioned view of Walter Benjamin, as well as earlier writings of William Morris, may be seen as an attempt to strategize with respect with the phenomenon of industrial mass production, driven by the 'antiquated' techno-capitalism of the 1930s. Aiming to fight against this inevitable feature of contemporary societies, that is to say, trying to recover the 'unique' characteristics of art "before the Age of Mechanic Reproduction", some artists took position against the novel characteristics of contemporary art, assuming the 'pessimistic' attitude of Adorno on the homo mechanicus. In regard to the linkage of art and society, the situationist critique may be seen as "the most radical gesture" (Plant, 1992) against the invasion of everyday life (Lefevbre, 1968) by Fordist (mis) conceptions, when industrialism made its appearance in the 'leisure' realm. In addition, public skepticism towards the military-industrial complex after May 1968, the Vietnam war, the mounting ecological concerns, all contributed to problematizing the artistic use of technology within the context of modern techno-capitalism. The Cybernetic Serendipity held in ICA, London, August-October 1968 – that may be viewed as the event that inaugurates the protohistory of computer-based art – marks also a turning point in the linkage of aesthetics to political contest. It is a curious coincidence that the starting of 'computer art' corresponds to the ending of the art/politics linkage.

The contemporary individual is no longer tied to any kind of transcendence (neither theological nor political). Hence, it is very intricate to invent a language that could express, through art, the ethos of this period, while remaining distinct from it. Moreover, the temporal acceleration of our times abolishes the gap between any 'subversive' avant-garde proposition and its social appropriation by the media, publicity and the like. Furthermore, in contrast with previous intellectual pursuits, the achievements of contemporary culture are not marginaldisputes between any group of "happy few", but affect the lives of everybody on the planet. This leads to a generalized aesthetic obsolescence of artworks – these are rapidly and easily 'transduced' into some kind of merchandise. Nowadays, art is everywhere, as artists always wished (even in commercial products and in decentralized 'mediatic' and 'mobile' exhibitions that fly from one country to another). What is important in contemporary art has nothing to do with the object that is produced, but with the underlying creative process: indeed, what the artist does is to reprocess ideas 'extracted' from his Zeitgeist.

Hence, as Duchamp put it, "everybody can be an artist", in the vein of the "self-proclamation theory". As an example of this, the "Society of Independent Artists, Inc", founded in 1916 in New York with Duchamp's involvement, accepted as a member anyone who pays a fee and exhibits an artwork, without indicating how artists are recognized as such, since exhibiting was no problem, given the famous rule "No jury, no prizes".

Since the contemporary world is driven by the information/

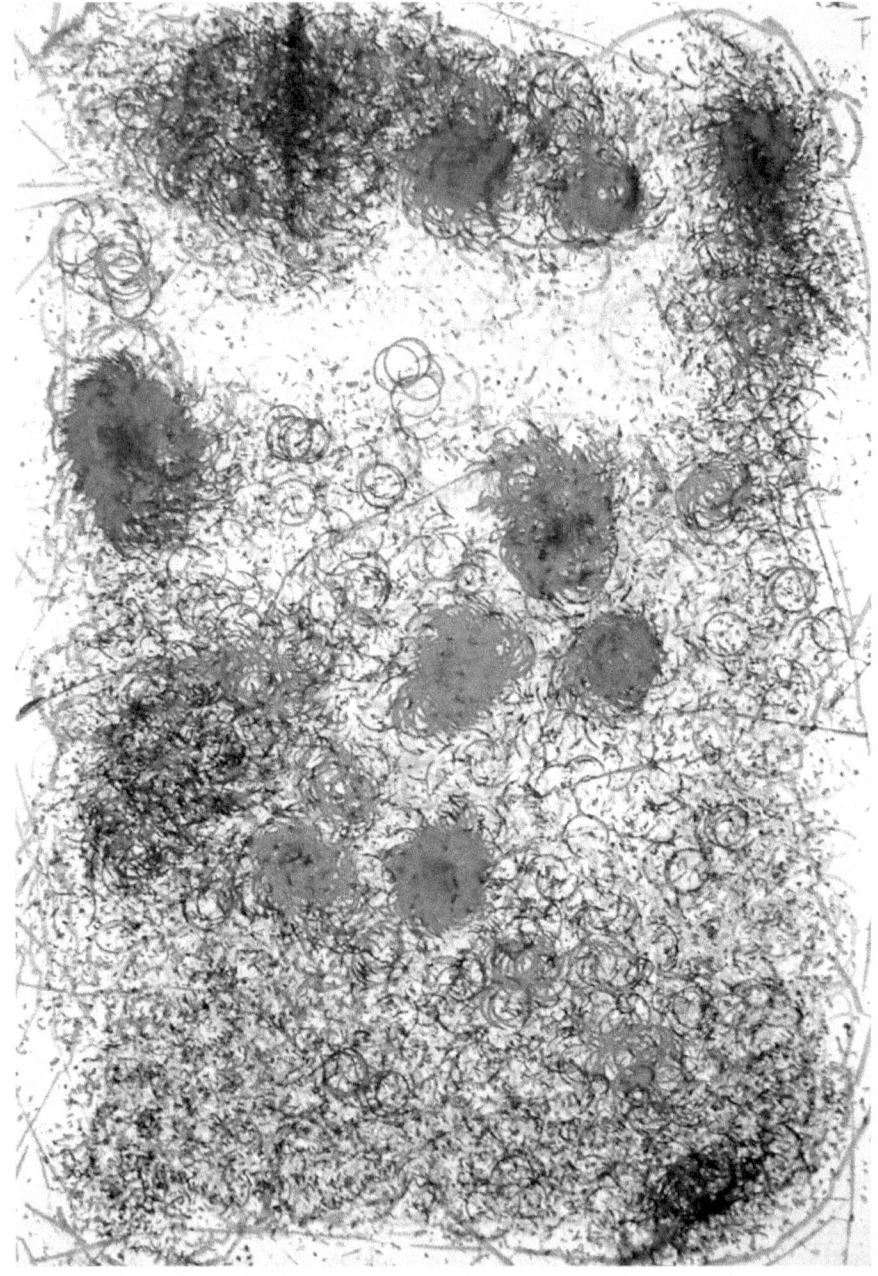

010304, 2004, acrylic on canvas, 195 x 130 cm

communication revolution, it is not astonishing that the art of our times has became 'digital' (and that 'digital' corporations like HP take possession of art, instead of Museum curator's or particular collection owners).

Art and philosophy

Since Kant asked the question "Was ist Aufklärung?" – that is, what was his own actuality – philosophy gained a new dimension. According to Foucault, this new dimension is to tell us who we are in terms of the present we are living in. By this 55 token, a new relationship between philosophy and contemporary art emerges. It is obvious that contemporary art has nothing to do with 'truth'. This is in sharp opposition to Heidegger's solemn claims, in the sequel of Foucaults's point of view that truth elicits power, and of Derrida's critique of the 'transcendent signified' as a unitary source of truth. Since 'truth' is inevitably distorted, Duchamp twists it further for himself for the fun of it, forgetting some things and selectively modifying or misrecollecting others. For instance, he performs the détournement of Jules Lefebvre "La verité" by inserting a mannequin feebly holding her lamp aloft inside his "Etant données".

However, having reached the current state of affairs where anything can be "art", the point is to confront the philosophical questions raised by artistic production. In Derrida's 1978 text "La verité en peinture", he asks the reader what would be his reaction to the putative impossibility of putting a frame in his artworks. And all Derridean analysis of art is always focused on the issue of the "frame" (how to bound the space of the oeuvre).

What is important in contemporary art is the interpretative plan, which gives meaning to artistic objects. As noted by Arthur Danto, contemporary art brings to an end its former search for essence, emphasizing its extensive, rather than intensive character. Once vanished all its intensive conditions, "art is now the totality of life" (Danto, 1997). The same seems to apply to hypertext, where extension prevails over intension (Pereira, 2002). The concept of 'expanded art', used by Valie Export as a collage extended in time and multiple space and media layers, may also be analysed under this perspective (Valie Export, 2003).

But, some decades before, situationists had already envisaged a society not merely of 'plenty' but of outright excess. In particular, Constant – with his New Babylon project that is an infinite container for mass-produced environments, fabulous technologies, and endless artistic exchange – puts forward a similar idea: "New Babylon ne s'arréte nulle part (puisque la Terre est ronde); elle ne connait point de frontiéres (puisque il

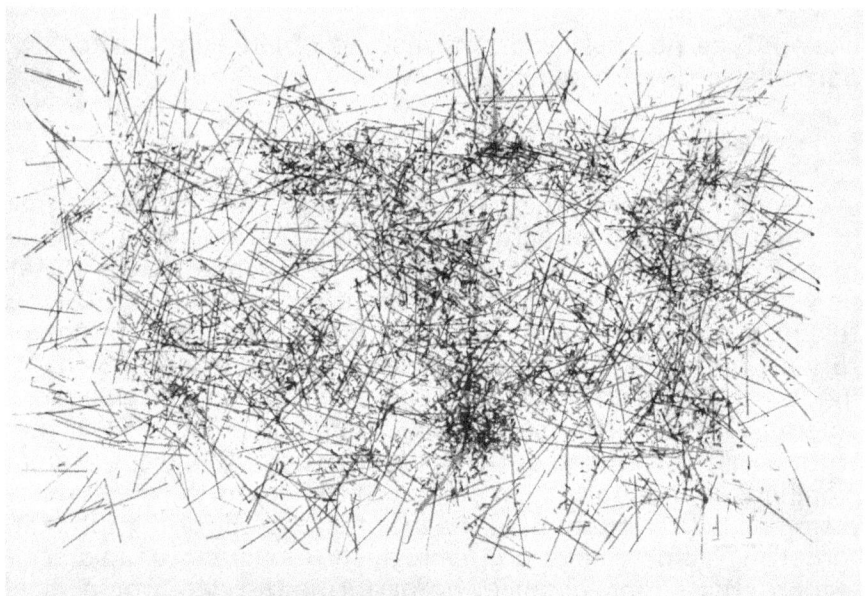

010504, 2004, ink on paper, 140 x 200 cm

n'y a pas d'ecónomies nationales, ni de collectivités (puisque l'humanité est flutuante)".

In fact, this rethoric of excess has a magnifying effect that may be spotted in the roots of the ArtSBot project positive feedback, but that can hardly be reached by conventional painting.

As reported by Pierre Cabanne in 1968, Duchamp's aim consisted above all in "forgetting the hand", inflating his artistic objects by embedding them in language. Hence, it is not surprising that most artists since then do not deal with conventional artworks, but with conceptual thinking.

Penny, 1995, claims that the 'Cultural Software' of contemporary aesthetics is represented by 'Conceptual Art'. In reality, the obvious striking parallels between Conceptual Art and developments in systems theory and computer information processing were disclosed by several authors (e.g. Shanken, 2001).

For Arthur Danto, the role of philosophy is to remove the artist's hand from the processes of art, as claimed by Duchamp, who was interested in an entirely cerebral art. For instance, in order to explain by discourse Duchamp's Fountain, it is not required to 'see' the object; a photo does the job.

The roots of such a discourse about art are found in the Greek ekphrasis, the verbal description of art works. Diderot made of this kind of narratives a literary canon, aimed at 'explaining' to the public (and art patrons ...) his contemporary painter's tableaux, for instance, La Tempête.

The relationship linking the artwork to all discourses that it evokes is also a concern of Derrida, namely in his consideration of the 'double bind' brought by the movement of the discourse to the intrinsic immobility of the artwork (Derrida, 1980).

The connection between art and linguistics is an important development where Antoni Muntadas – who emphasised the importance of 'translation' in conceptually artistic terms – pursues Umberto Eco's approach on Opera Aperta. In fact, Muntadas considers translation as incorporating not only languages but also different media and different technologies. His open work, contains different levels of possible interpretation of how languages are transcribed into/onto each other (Muntadas, 2003).

Some views of Kierkegaard and Nietzsche on 'difference and repetition', as interpreted by Deleuze, 1994, may be seen as predecessors of contemporary art, considered as an open field of possibilities where critical standards do not rely on any kind of ideology. In fact, those views favour difference over identity, as opposed to the classical philosophical scrutiny of artworks (from Plato to Hegel), based on their characteristics of uniqueness that stems from authorship authority.

In this regard, it is worth stressing the multiplicity of instances produced by ArtSBot, which can be seen as realizations of a random function, showing "how things might be otherwise". In artistic terms, this means that artworks, being by nature ephemeral and incomplete, contain a certain common feature: they are the present as a moment of becoming ("life as it is" turns into "life as it could be"). The emergence of an artwork stems from the organized spontaneity that contains two apparently antagonistic features: the random and the 'aquis'. For Duchamp, this corresponds to his paroxysmal search for "alternatives" and, for Constant, this apparent paradox reveals the coherence of the artist that accepts unpredictability.

On the other hand, the concept of 'diagram', as exposed by Deleuze's reading of Foucault (Deleuze, 1988), is a good framework for understanding, in philosophical terms, the conceptual foundation of contemporary art. In fact, this 'abstract machine', as opposed to any transcendent Idea and to any kind of economic infrastructure à la Marx, is the instable and fluent mapping of a series of relationships that give rise to a new entity by a self-organizing process leading to a sudden 'cooperation' between previously disconnected elements, when a critical point is reached.

Given the value Magritte placed on thought, it is not surprising that his work has drawn the attention of philosophers like Foucault since the 1960s (e.g. Foucault, 1968). But the ideas that are behind Magritte's interaction with Foucault could be capable of becoming visible only through painting, supporting Foucault's proposal of 'art' as a multiplicity of parts that are both theoretical and practical, against the canonical 'conceptual art' that separates theory from practice. Along these lines, it is worth noting that Magritte is a marvellous inventor of forms, for whom a "false true" value in logic can have a profound aesthetic reality in art. This example, taken from an important art practitioner, illustrates the trivial claim that art 'has nothing to do' with classical logic. In complexity theory terms, it can be stated that bifurcating states of permutation are transposed into self-similarity. Also, it is worth noting that contemporary art practice is unimaginable without appealing to the deconstruction concept à la Derrida. This point reaches its pinnacle with neo-conceptualism, which is no more than a distillation of the deconstructive method.

Recombining art, science and philosophy

under a new dissenting perspective – unmanned art

The new dissenting perspective in political terms, which opposes to the old idea of a sudden revolution that changes life overnight, is represented for instance by the Italian group called "Tutte Bianche". This group is inspired by the Zapatista movement and appeared in Milan in 1994 during the 'anti-globalisation' fights. The name that was adopted was an ironic response to the epithet of 'ghosts' that the Mayor of Milan assigned to squatters. In the line of Marcos' dictum "we don't know what to do with a vanguard that cannot be reached by anybody", they intend to be submerged in the 'multitude'. They mix the 'imaginary' with the material basis of political criticism, the underground with the mainstream, high culture with popular culture (which in Latin languages means "made by the people").

This type of 'movement' focus on the breaking of all dualistic oppositions (like visibility/non-visibility, legality/non-legality, violence/nonviolence before/after the revolution...) by dividing all united things and approximating all separated things, for the sake of the creation of strange feelings of nearness and distance.

The 'culture jam' that occurs in the 'antiglobalisation' groups is a novel characteristic of our times, in sharp contrast with the 'goaldirected' avantguardistic attitude based on some kind of 'identity' that prevailed during fights against Fordist capitalism.

This complex union of stability and chaos may be interpreted as a fractal phenomenon, where strange attractors maintain a certain unity, despite all turbulence.

Along these lines, Perniola, 1994, proposes a porous way of thinking which does not anchor itself within methodological safe limits. In fact, Perniola puts forward the idea of transit, the trespassing of one thing into another, of one field of knowledge into another, without ever defining the borders between internal and external limits. From the work of Perniola, one can draw the concept of the thing who feels, the thing that plays, and, a fortiori, the thing – the group of robots – that interacts with the environment in an arty way. This line of thought can be derived from the original idea of Asger Jorn that individual creativity can not be explained purely in terms of psychic phenomena. In his critique of Breton's surrealism, Jorn made the point that explication is itself a physical act which materializes thought, and so psychic automatism is closely joined to physical automatism (Jorn, 2001). What is surprising is that this attitude goes along the fresh approach developed recently by Rodney Brooks in the field of robotics. Conversely, it is worth noting how Brooks's approach influenced computer-based art in its 'materialization' aspect (at least, since the 1993 Ars Electronica Conference, cf. Shanken, 2001). In fact, the MIT researcher considers that human nature can be seen to possess the essential characteristics of a machine, even though this idea is usually rejected instinctively by our putative uniqueness, stemming from some kind of "tribal specialness" (Brooks, 2002). In parallel, Derrida criticizes the usual neglect of non-human actors in "Il n'y a pas d'hors-text" (Derrida, 1967) and, in "Papier Machine", he shows how a text (Rousseau's Confessions) can function machinalement, i.e., by itself, emancipated from the author and even cut from him.

Similarly, William Carlos Williams considers "a poem as a small (or large) machine made of word".

Duchamp had already put in practice the same idea in his 1926-1927 "Large Glass". This is a "machine moved by a proverb – it's the words that make the machine run" (Suquet, 1992). In his unsigned "Green Box", Duchamp put together the legend to "Large Glass": ninety four scraps of paper bearing plans, drawings, hastily jotted notes, and freely drawn rough drafts were delivered in bulk.

In the scope of ArtSBot, it can be stated that if an idea becomes a machine that makes the art, then there is no point in immitating Nature, but to perceive the "beauty of the idea" (Le Witt, 1967). If a self-referential art that does not care for objects is to be made, then the point is to simulate those artificial features of life (as it could be) that are driven by creativity. And creativity, as Debord put it as early as 1957, is not the capacity of arranging objects and forms, it is the invention of new laws on that arrangement. Hence, the point is no more to create objects, not even 'contexts' in Duchamp's terms.

Now, in unmanned art, not only the artwork depends on the idea that generated it, but a complete symbiosis occurs between the artist and the machine.

Human and robot bodies are ultimately related to a common ground: Deleuze & Guattari's "Machine phylum". In the late 1960s Deleuze realized the philosophical implications of three levels of the phase space where man and machines co-evolve. These are specific trajectories, corresponding to objects in the real world; attractors, corresponding to the long term tendencies of those objects; and bifurcations, corresponding to spontaneous mutations occurring in those objects (Deleuze & Guattari, 1980).

The human behind the idea is the Symbiotic Artist, the one who brings about the conditions for 'situations' to be constructed.

BIOART
[2004]

Bioart is a new kind of biological inspired art that campaigns for the emergence of a new artificial, dynamic and self-sustainable Nature. Hence, the main point is to generate life as an artistic expression (but not life as it is, rather life as it could be). In such a feature, this new kind of art departs radically from the (sad) idea of using human and animal bodies transformed in art works, as well as from the practice of employing organic materials in the pieces and installations that have plagued 20th century museums and art galleries.

The distinctiveness of this new kind of art may be addressed in the following five topics:

Creation is viewed in the sense that bioart does not want just to represent or imitate Nature but seeks to build the conditions for a new Nature to emerge, an artificial one (or a manipulated one in some instances). Even if criticism, always welcomed, can say that we are still very far from that, it is clear that bioartists aim to do exactly that: to create an artificial Nature to be regarded as an artistic expression that supplements natural Nature.

Combination is an essential aspect of scientific and cultural innovation. However, in the case of bioart, synergy, blending and recombination are mechanisms that are not only present at the level of the research, but on the origin of the concept. In contrast with many previous artistic tendencies where the "scientific" served as an external reference or as a means to stimulate imagery, bioart is as much art as it is science. In order to produce bioartworks, artists need to become themselves scientists.

Symbiosis as interspecies cooperation is at work in many and diverse ways in bioart (sometimes between man and other living creatures, in most cases between man and smart machines). Man-machine interaction and cooperation is one bioart's most outstanding aspects. Art, because it is free from purpose and predetermined goals, plays an important cultural and scientific role in the process of developing intelligent machines.

Far from the fitness constraints so common in the military, industrial or even entertainment applications, man-machine cooperation in art is purely creative, i.e., a contingent trial and error process that generates truly autonomous new artificial beings.

Randomness is part of the adaptive behavior. In the human species art and culture are adaptive behaviors based on randomness. Considering the culture in which we live as our environment, we use art to evolve and adapt. But adaptation here means that the artist does not seek a solution for any problem. He just makes things run and sees what happens.

Bioart introduces some relevant changes in the millenarian process of adaptation. For the first time in human culture, art is not just interpreting or redesigning nature, but seeking to use the biological random mechanism to originate a new kind of Nature.

Post-humanity is an important issue in bioart, since it contributes to liberate the human species from a putative neurotic superiority that has given rise to such a perverse and massacring relation with the rest of living beings. In bioart the human narrative, so tediously exploited in mainstream contemporary art, is rarely a subject. Bioartists are mainly interested in the mechanisms of life, rather than in typical human moralistic approaches. In this context, to know that the human is as important as, for example, a small ant is a crucial point (and for those working with swarm intelligence the ant behavior can be much more stimulating and rewarding).

These five topics on bioart are enough to demonstrate that a new kind of art is emerging. In some features, it is plain art as we know it, rebellious, ingenious and innovative. But its cultural environment is very distinct from the ongoing debate on contemporary art, which is too focused on anthropocentric non-problems. And that is perhaps the main reason why this new kind of art, now already present in the academic and scientific domain, is taking so long to reach a wider public in the art world. Anyway, les jeux sont faits.

THE END OF ART AS WE KNOW IT
[2005]

The Painting Robots were created to paint. Not my paintings but their own paintings. Such an objective may seem simple but in fact it adresses some of the most critical ideas on art, robotics and artificial intelligence. Let me start with intelligence.

Today we understand intelligence as a basic feedback mechanism. If a system, any system, is able to respond to a certain stimulus in a way that it changes itself or its environment we can say that some sort of intelligence is present. *Sheer* intelligence is therefore something that doesn't need to refer to any kind of purpose, target or quantification. It may plainly be an interactive mechanism of any kind, with no other objective than to process information and to react in accordance to available output capabilities.

Yet this is not what we usually observe in most of the artificial intelligence undertakings. For one part because human intelligence is still seen as the *great* model to be followed and by which all the experiments should be measured and evaluate. Artificial intelligence is in general a shadow of what we believe to be the human mind and behavior.

As opposed to this, the painting robots were built without any previous intelligence model, human or other. The idea was to make an artificial being able to do paintings without any external reference or requirements. That is why I don't use fitness constraints or optimization parameters. It is the simple mechanism of feedback and stigmergy that is at work here. Such a project cannot be evaluated in terms of any kind of human accomplishment or natural behavior.

The painting robots are nothing more than a singular species, with a particular form of intelligence and a kind of life of its own. They do paintings as other species build nests, change habitats or create social affiliations.

Viewed simply as robots, i.e. autonomous and intelligent machines, they are also distinct from the *mainstream*. Their aim is not to simulate animal behavior or any type of classical embodied process. All the parts that they are made of, and all the actions they are able to perform derive from the single purpose

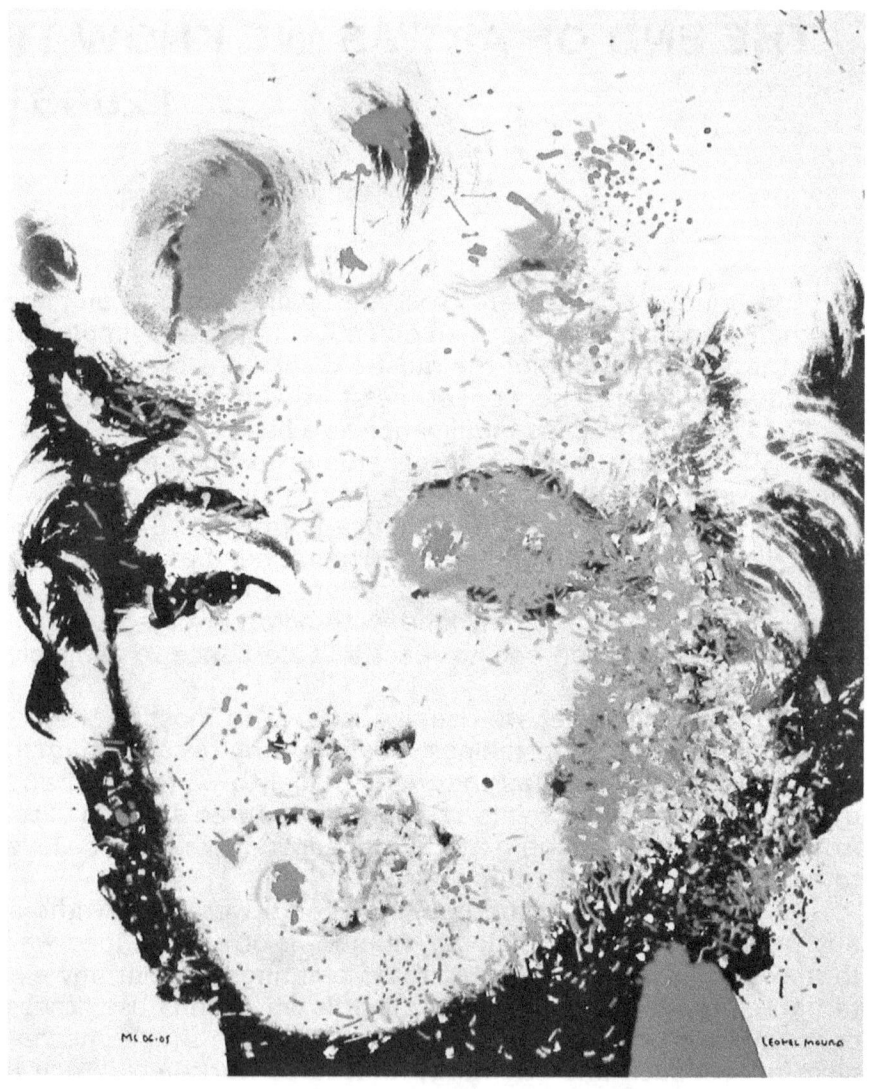

Erased Marilyn 0605, 2005, ink and acrylic on canvas, 100 x 80 cm

of making their own paintings. That is why they have visual sensors in order to recognize colors, wheels to move, a brain to process information and a device to paint. Even the decorative aspect was brought to a minimum. The painting robots were specifically created as a new form of life dedicated to the production of paintings. Not more not less.

If robots would appreciated art, the Painting Robots artworks would probably be the ones they would liked most. They are a true intelligent machine expression. But, since we, humans, are for the time being the only meditative observers, the relation between machine art and human aesthetics perception is of great interest. I believe that we don't fully understand these paintings. Complexity is easy to explain but not so easy to grasp when we see it at work. Anyway, many of us like the paintings, probably because we seem to gladly embrace fractal or chaotic structures. But, more than shapes and colors, what some of us really like here is the idea and the associated process. In this sense, these robotic paintings are a provocative conceptual art that problematizes the boundaries of art as we know it.

In my practical experience with these robots I have generally fed them with a blank canvas and color pens choosen at random. But sometimes I have also provided a canvas already painted with a previous image, a seed, which the robots take as a starting point to create a superimposed composition. In the human eye's perspective, this looks like a correction or comment on the given image, even if the robots never sees the whole of it, reacting only to local information. Our interpretation of the final painting is thus affected by the common gestalt mechanism and more strongly by moral, political or aesthetical aspects that are completely out of the process. In this sense, these particular paintings are a very good metaphor of our intrinsic difficulty to relate with intelligent machine behavior (or any kind of information that does not derive from our own cognitive models).

In the series where I have use Warhol's Marilyn as a seed, this issue is clearly raised. The robots just react to an environment with much defined contrasts. Therefore they are prone to paint over the more graphic shapes, as mouth or eyes. This, for us, constitutes a profanation of the portrait, a kind of an iconoclastic statement that arises the terrific vision of a world dominated by destructive machines.

In conclusion, I am not aiming to build domesticated robots (and it is not by accident that one of the most current well-known robot it's a dog...) but, on the contrary, I will currently keep on trying to create intelligent and autonomous machines dedicated to its own life and art. In fact I don't see the Marilyn Seed paintings as a destructive manifesto, but instead as the positive construction of a new kind of art or as I like to put it: The End Of Art As We Know It and the opening of a vast field of artistic experiments - human and non-human.

A NEW ART PARADIGM [2007]

It seems to me that no one in the world has ever made something this beautiful and important.
Escher

Robotics endorses, among other things, the overcome of the worn out paradigm of the so-called contemporary art. In the last decades arts suffered a conceptual erosion process by focusing on a strong individualistic subjectivism, justified by market effects that are not very distinct from generic merchandise promotion. Too much money, too short talent and abundant meaningless works keep the deceiving excitement and the glamour, typical of the fashion effects. The most common themes are based on small tricks of prestidigitation, exacerbating trivial personalities or detaching variations from processes carried out a long time ago, but under different context and scope. And as William Burroughs reminded: "the essence of the prestidigitation is the distraction and the wrong information". Duchamp's contextualization technique continues to prevail in many works, with nothing being added to the original gesture of Marcel Duchamp. Out of the museums and art galleries many works are totally irrelevant and reduced to their real condition of garbage.

A reboot is required.

Art and technology are historical partners. In Renaissance the camera obscura and the optics opened the doors of perspective in painting. Later, the industrial revolution and photography led to an increasing autonomy of the work of art and gave rise to abstraction. Nowadays, the computer, the Internet and biological driven concepts expand the art to the fields of posthumanity and postnature.

Computers proved to be much more than a sophisticated word processor and fast calculator. They are a powerful mean to think, design and materialize. The computer is a partner in the creation of ideas and processes. It is a machine that extends our brain and helps thinking the unimaginable. It is something that stimulates our brain, allowing to derive and test in the twinkling of an eye, multiple hypotheses, many of them impossible to achieve by our own means. Computer is a prosthetic augmentation of the mind.

The Internet transformed knowledge into an immersive experience. It made accessible, free and workable from anywhere in the globe many skills, which until shortly were only available to elites. In a logic of freeware and open source, this enormous conveyor of knowledge stimulates, extends and expands human intelligence by generating at any time new knowledge, in an endless cycle. The Internet is an accelerator of the cultural evolution.

Biology wide opened the door to life. No other science is nowadays so influential, so crucial in terms of future, so fascinating and at the same time so terrifying. The descent to the most basic principles of life revealed how things work. And, as opposed to the expected linear mechanisms, complexity and emergent processes were found. Hence the need for experimentation. Certain facts can only be configured when triggered. Complexity, emergence and self-organization became central concepts to describe many processes all around, since the formation of galaxies to the manifestation and development of life.

The discovery of the Genome deciphered the deepest mechanism driving the way how all living organisms in the planet work, by revealing the enormous complexity of an essentially random process, from which emerges the order that we recognize in bodies and behaviors. Genome also allowed the beginning of a new type of manipulation of the living, putting an end to Darwin's evolutionism. The evolution of many animals, plants and mankind, is now the product of biotechnology and does not rely anymore on the slow process of trial and error that nature elaborates since millions of years. From this enterprise extraordinary beings and horrible monstrosities will be born. Mankind will be forced to rephrase conceptually almost everything, since our role in the universe, to deep ethical questions. In a more immediate plan this new way of thinking must assure openness, sharing and free recombination of knowledge. Freeware and open source concepts are to become the main model of socialization.

Art is an environment transformer. In the new context of technocreative production, art is so influenced by technology as it exerts an enormous influence on it. The so-called New Technologies are the result of creative and artistic minds, as well as from a libertarian impulse characteristic of artists. The encounter of art with science and technology is more than a simple

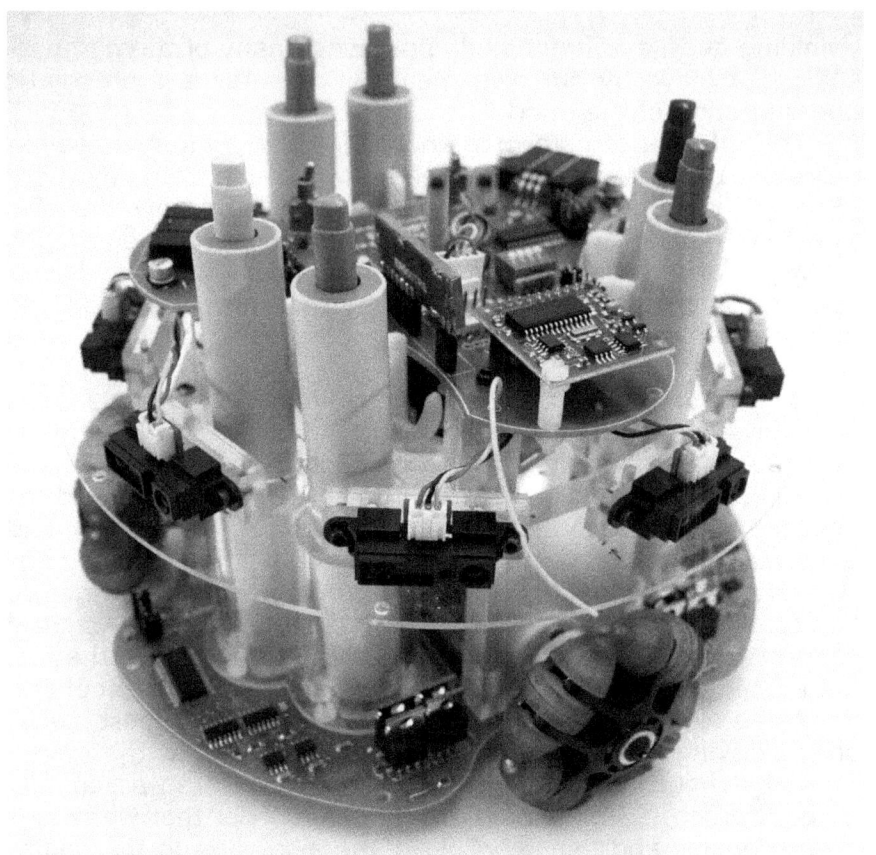

RAP, Robotic Action Painter, 2006

opportunist and functional joint venture. The recombination of ideas from art, science and technology generates more art, science and technology, leading to a unstoppable dynamics.

But art is also, itself, an evolutionary mechanism. Essentially trial and error based, random, mutant and stochastic.

Hence it reveals itself as complementary to science. Because art is always true, unlike science that is only true until proven otherwise, it is allowed to explore all corners of the imaginary and parts of the unimaginable. That process increases the creativity field, which is today only limited by ignorance and practical unfeasibility. Enhancing intelligence is therefore an important issue for art, as well, of course, for humanity.

Bioart, biological inspired art, is a perfect terrain for this exploration of art and science recombination. In fact, viewing it as a mere scientific illustration is to be shortsighted. The generation and manipulation of living organisms, regarded as an artistic expression, is really transbiological since it intends to exceed the borders of life as we know it. This kind of art is merged with life as it could be and not as it is.

Such a process opens space for innovative recombinations of natural with artificial, living with metallic, electronic with neuronal, silicon with genetic. The new artificial, robotized, hybrid, symbiotic entities are agents of the ongoing reconfiguration of the planet. Artists can now put into practice the aesthetical society, as announced by philosophers and utopists. And this is performed, by morphogenesis, not by embellishing the world as it is now.

Hence, the new art paradigm can be defined by the concrete and deliberate construction of a new nature.

This haphazard arrangement of forms will be the future of artistic harmony.
Wassily Kandinsky

The mind as brain-at-work can be made visible.
E.O.Wilson

Based on ants and other social insect studies, I have tried to reproduce artificially a similar emergent behavior in a robot swarm. These insects communicate among themselves through chemical messages, the pheromones, based on which they produce certain patterns of collective behavior, like follow a trail, clean up, repair and build nests, defense, attack or territory conquest. Despite pheromone not being the exclusive way of communication among these insects - the touch of antennas in ants or the dance in bees are equally important -, pheromonal language produces complex cognition via bottom-up procedures. Pheromone expression is dynamic, making use of increments and decrements, positive and negative feedbacks. Messages are amplified when pheromone is reinforced, and lose "meaning" when breeze disperses it. It is also an indirect communication, coined stigmergy from the Greek stigma/sign and ergon/action. Between the individual who places the message and the one who is stimulated by it, there is no proximity or direct relation.

Following these principles, in my first ant-robots (2001) I have replaced pheromone by color. The marks left by one robot triggers a pictorial action on other robots. Through this appar-

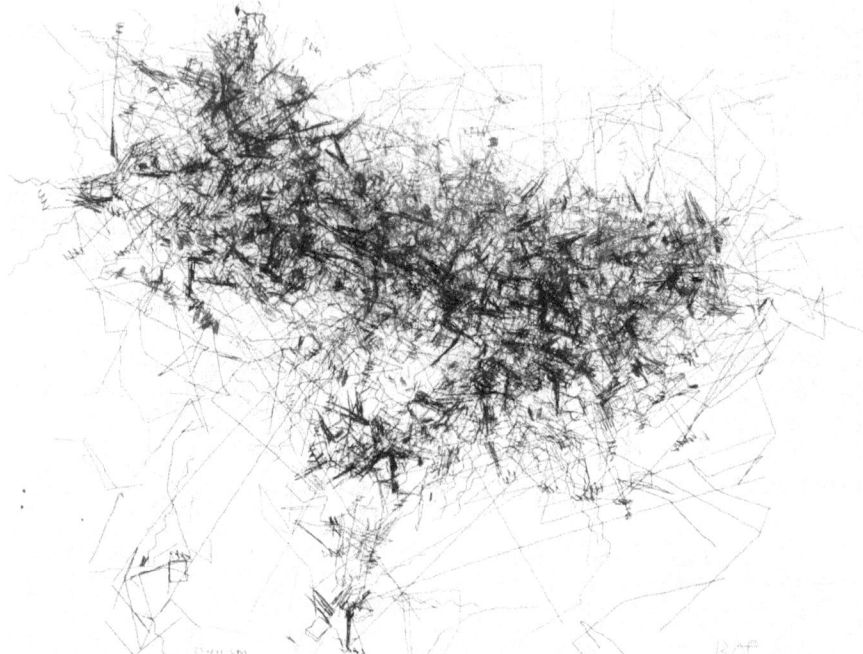

RAP, 230807, 2007, ink on canvas, 130 x 180 cm

ent random mechanism abstract paintings are generated, which reveal well defined shapes and patterns. My robots create abstract paintings that seem at first sight just random doodles, but after some reflexive observation color clusters and patterns become patent. Through the recognition of the color marks left by a robot, the others react to it reinforcing certain color spots.

The process is thus everything but arbitrary, stemming from a creative technique analogue to millions of years of evolution.

ArtSBot (Art Swarm Robots) was the first project to use emergent organization for developing robot creativity. Every previous experiment focused exclusively on randomness or sometimes on target strategies leading the machines to fulfill a predetermined program created by the human artist.

On the contrary, ArtSBot was ment to put into practice the utmost possible machine autonomy, aimed at producing original paintings.

In operational terms, ArtSBot consists of a series of small "turtle" type robots, equipped with two felt pens and a pair of RGB sensors pointing to the painting plan. With these "eyes" the robots seek color, determine if it is hot or cold, choose the corresponding pen and strengthen it by a constant or variable trace. To begin the process, when the canvas is still blank, the robots leave here and there a small spot of color randomly. Based on these simple rules, unique paintings are produced: from a random background stands out a well defined composition with intense shapes of color. In other words, initial randomness generates "order". The process is emergent and based on the properties of stigmergy.

The artistic product of these robots is entirely original. In the same way that somebody who writes a book cannot be considered as a mere instrument of his primary school teacher, robots cannot be seen as simple instruments of the artist that conceived and programmed them. There is an effective incorporation of new and non pre-determined information in the process. And that cannot be called anything but creativity.

It is true that consciousness is lacking to this creativity. But if we look at the history of modern art, it is obvious that, for example, surrealism tried to produce art works exactly in these same terms.

The "pure psychic automatism", the quintessential definition of the movement itself, appeared as a spontaneous, non-conscious and without any aesthetic or moral intention technique.

In the first Surrealist Manifesto André Breton defined the concept in this way: "Pure psychic automatism by which it is intended to express (…) the true function of thought. Thought dictated in the absence of all control exerted by reason and outside all aesthetic or moral preoccupations".

In the field of the visual arts, it is Pollock who better fulfills this intention by splashing ink onto the canvas with the purpose of representing nothing but the action itself. This was coined Action Painting, as it is well-known. Perhaps, because of that, the first paintings from my robots are, aesthetically, so similar to the ones of Pollock or André Masson, another important automatism based painter. In his surrealist period, this artist tried frequently to prompt a low conscious state by going hungry, not sleeping or taking drugs, so that he could release himself from any rational control and therefore letting emerge what at the time, in the path of Freud, was called the subconscious.

The absence of conscience, external control or pre-determination, allow my painting robots to engender creativity in its pure state, without any representational, aesthetic or moral intention.

RAP (Robotic Action Painter), created in 2006 for the Museum of Natural History in New York, is an individualist artist and not a swarm, but makes use of the same composition methods based on stigmergy and emergence. This robot is additionally able to determine, by its own means, the moment in which the painting is finished. Previous versions didn't have this capacity being conditioned by battery discharge or my will to stop the process. RAP's decision is taken based on the information that it gathers directly from the painting, what produces a considerable variation of time and form, since RAP can decide that the work is complete after a relatively short while (entailing accordingly a low pictorial expression) or can extend the picture construction for a quite long period, making it much more dense and complex. The "secret" of this behavior is in the significant change of the sensors, which passed from two to nine "eyes", allowing now the reading of local patterns, in addition to color spots. RAP is also my first robot to sign its works.

ISU, the poet robot also created in 2006, has the ability to write letters and words producing poems and emergent compositions based on the letter, quite similarly to the Lettrism style, artistic movement that followed Surrealism.

These references to 20th century art movements do not seek any kind of historical legitimacy, but are intended simply to show how certain morphogenesis processes produce similar results in human as well as non-human artists.

My painting robots generate art works based on emergence. The essential of those creations is based on the machine own interpretation of the world and not on its human description. No previous plan, fitness, aesthetical taste or artistic model is induced. The robots are just machines dedicated to their art.

Creativity is not an exclusive ability of human culture and it can be acknowledge in the same way in the physical, biological and artificial world.

ANTENNAE INTERVIEW
[2009]

We would like to thank you for the opportunity to pose these
questions, the complexities of which reflect the challenging na-
ture of your work. By way of introduction, can you describe how
you came to be interested in robotics as an artistic medium, and
the process by which you conceived the robots in relationship
to animals?

I have always been a conceptual artist, but by mid 1990's I thought that the so-called "contemporary art" was burned out. The dissemination of the Personal Computer and the Internet made clear that art need radical change. Not since artists would now have new tools, but because these new tools fuelled deep implications in knowledge and creativity. Science as changed a lot in the last decades, art not so much. For the first time in history art is staying behind.

This delay stems from some kind of resistance of "humanities" against scientific thought. It is common for artists to utter anti-technological statements that they pretend to be a defence of humans. But in fact they just reflect ignorance and superstition not very dissimilar from religious irrationalism.

In this context I became more and more interested in architecture and science. I have started working with algorithms to generate "buildings" which was feasible in the virtual world but not in the real one. These first rather frustrating experiments helped to define better the new field of interests. Morphogenesis, intelligence and autonomy appeared to me as the key concepts to generate intelligent and autonomous agents able to create their own artworks. Robots were the unavoidable choice.

Later on - to answer to the second part of your question - I started looking at robots as a new species evolving to colonize

Questions by Paula Lee
These questions grew out of a conversation between myself, an art historian/
historian of science, and my collaborator Anat Pollack, who is an interactive
media installation artist. She should be credited as co-interviewer.

our planet. Although robots are frequently meant to mimic animals - by simulating behaviours and appearances –, I see them as a distinct species.

In the post-Cartesian history of modern robotics, "the animal" has served as a model for mechanical systems rather than as part of an embedded environment linked to survival strategies and behaviours. Do you see your robots as challenges to this formulation?

When we shift from the animal as a mechanical model to life as an autopoietic system, we understand that it is not so important to simulate mechanics but rather to trigger self-sustained processes. If we speak about autonomous robots, the question – as Christopher Langton put it – is not life-as-it-is but rather life as-it-could-be.

Let me give the example of the famous – but lost – Vaucanson mechanical duck constructed in the 18th century. This duck seemly could eat and defecate. But the simulation of digestion was in fact nothing more than a clever magic trick, consisting of discarding some kind of pre-prepared material, which looks like faeces.

The most interesting autonomous robots of today are bio-inspired but what they do is not an illusion. It is the real thing.

In 2006, for the Museum of Natural History in New York, you created a work that featured RAP ("robot action painter") who was also able to sign its own creations. How much randomness in a process (albeit a programmed randomness) removes the hand of the programmer? At what point does the robot become that which is no longer you or yours, and thus capable of authorship?

My problem was how to build a system able to generate autonomously original and distinctive paintings. Hence, decisive in this robot is not randomness, but its ability to gather by itself the information it needs to build a pictorial composition. What you call the "hand of the programmer" is meant to provide decision making skills, not to give precise instructions.

In this case, it is adequate to put forward the issue of artificial creativity, meaning the ability of a machine to simulate human or animal creativity, but showing also some characteristics of its own (I make an analogy between artificial intelligence as an ontological property and artificial creativity).

One of these characteristics stems from stigmergy. Stigmergy is a form of indirect communication through the environment. The robot only "sees" a small and local part of the painting – the environment – , but that information is enough to generate an original composition that it is not random but also not deterministic. Hence the author of such a composition is obviously the robot, using some kind of creativity that does not depend on the human action that has launched the process.

A core question posed by the affirmation of the animal as artist (the bee as architect, the bowerbird as builder, the beaver as engineer, the dolphin as dancer, the elephant as painter, etc.), is also provoked by your robots: does must art be informed by intentionality, consciousness, and historicity on the part of the maker, or is the (human) audience's capacity to provide these elements both a necessary and sufficient requirement to the conditions of art-making? Put another way: can robots be spectators? Does it matter if the robots, like the rabbits in Watership Down, neither know nor care to call the shapes they're making "art"?

Intentionality and consciousness are not indispensable concepts when we speak about morphogenesis. Termites don't know that they are building their impressive Termitaria. My robots don't have any idea who Pollock was. Anyway, we humans can appreciate what Termites or RAP do, as aesthetical, artistic or creative constructions.

The distinction between human art and animal or machine art is the result of the anthropocentric ideology that has always dominated human religion and philosophy. My work tries to express a critical view to that perspective by making the point that creativity – like intelligence – is inherent to all living organisms, including the artificial ones.

As a way to contextualize robot art, many of your writings invoke Surrealism's exploration of "pure psychic automatism" as affirmed by André Breton. However, a closer analogy to the totality of the installations might be Duchamp's demonstrations of "controlled chance," an experiment later taken up by American avant-garde artists such as choreographer Merce Cunningham. Cunningham's dancers followed movements he patterned but were mutually indifferent; they were free to do what they wanted as long as they stayed on stage, their actions thus defined by the parameters he had set out for them. Your robot installations would seem to inherit the legacy of performance art in an age where chaos theory seeks to complicate linear models of mechanistic determinism. Would you agree with this observation, and if not, why?

I have quoted several times the surrealist concept of "pure psychic automatism" just to demonstrate that art can be made minimizing consciousness. But I wouldn't speak about a "controlled chance" here, because the real issue is precisely to "lose control".

Though randomness and determinism – like positive feedback and thresholds – are present in my algorithms, what really matters for the outcome is stigmergy and emergence.

Historian of science Minsoo Kang has noted the robot's "uncanny" ability to blur structural binaries such as human/animal, man/woman, and other artifacts of human culture influentially described by anthropologist Claude Lévi-Strauss. Even as your robots gray the area between man and (other) animals, does this open up the eventual possibility that they will rely on neither for meaning?

I am absolutely convinced that the more robots will become autonomous, the more they will establish their own kind of behaviour, intelligence, creativity (and even individual and collective goals). Some will appear to be familiar to us, in the same way that we tend to anthropomorphize animals and objects. But some will gain distinctiveness and novelty to the point of becoming incomprehensible to us. We will need to build a new science dedicated to the comprehension of robots' behaviour. It could be coined Robotology if the name wasn't already spoiled by a youngster television series.

We pose here, something like a chicken and an egg problem: your writings affirm the robots as a new "species," and link their response habits to those demonstrated by social insects such as ants. It is arguably to that insecta in general that your robots bear the most physical resemblance. But is it necessary to understand robots through principles of resemblance in the first place? Are your machines meant to mirror biological processes in some way, or is this a corollary expression of other factors?

My model is not based on insects in general but specifically on eusocial insects, such as ants, bees or termites. These particular species have developed a unique kind of social organization based on simple rules, stigmergy, cooperation and labour specialization. I took inspiration from some of these characteristics, aiming at performance rather than resemblance.

In fact autonomous robots are still at the stage of a kind of Cambrian Explosion period. From all the current morphologies and behaviours, a few will evolve and most will perish. And of course we have not yet been able to introduce any kind of replication, a sine qua non condition for the robots to achieve their own evolution and "biology".

Engineers have created digital evolutionary systems that solve problems in ways humans have never considered, partly because of the ability of machines to process tremendous amounts of calculations without pause. To what extent do you believe that "robots will soon acquire their own freewill and be detached from us?" Is this a poetic notion, or is it truly believed that robots can exist in parallel to humans as autonomous agents?

With my robot RAP I have introduced a kind of freewill, given that it is the machine that decides when the work is finished. This is not done with a quantitative threshold - like time or amount of strokes -, but with a "perceptive" observation of the painting status.

If the issue is true autonomy, some kind of freewill must be present. It does not mean, necessarily, our kind of conscious freewill but instead, the ability of a machine to make unpredicted decisions.

Your robot zoo, Robotarium, is a fascinating work, not only because the zoo model fetishizes by excision and isolation, implying that robot life is in need of protection, but it also thus signals that humans and robots are competing for status and resources, and humans are winning. Is Robotarium a form of activism, one that calls attention to our collective limitations, implying that the mutual survival of humans and other creatures depends on competition for finite resources? How much of the "art" here resides in the need and desire our brains have to seek order in the chaos, and the poetic in the ordinary? Is survival of the (robot) species postulated, and if so, how would this affect the politically-charged discourse of species and specieism?

NONHUMAN ART

In fact the Robotarium spreads some flavour of domination, given that the robots are imprisoned inside a cage for human observation. But I would emphasize that our curiosity towards a distinct form of life is the first step for acceptance and respect. In this sense, I advocate an extension of the ecological awareness to include machines. Actually machines are already an essential component of our ecosystem. It is unthinkable for us to live without them. And terrible boring too.

In Electric Animal, Akira Mizura Lippit posits the animal as a kind of already-undead being, one that is caught in a state of perpetual vanishing due to the incursions of language. The Robotarium might seem to be a commentary on, and a hastening of, the vanishing of animals. Insofar as living animals are going extinct at an alarming rate, do you see your robots as positive successors filling the subsequent void, or as potential simulacrum hastening the "irrelevance" of carbon-based life?

The fact is that my mind does not work that way. I don't see robots with a minus but with a plus sign. We have humans, birds, fish, bees and now we must add robots.

Robots will certainly replace humans and other animals in many tasks and ways, but not inevitably in the context of natural life extermination, which is a direct consequence of human behaviour.

Anyhow, it is not very interesting to look at the rise of robots as a fictional conflict between artificial and natural life. More fascinating is to focus on the various forms of hybridization that are already occurring and will, for sure, increase greatly in the near future. The boundary between artificial and natural is not operative anymore. Just look at the so-called wildlife animals which are walking with a GPS collar around their neck, and cannot survive without the permanent human protection and assistance. Wildlife is now so much natural as it is artificial.

Hybridization affects bodies, minds, behaviours and also common destiny. We cannot see it just as prosthesis. For example, the role of our first partner in space exploration – the dog Laika -, is now being played by robots. Space exploration will only be possible with the combination of human/robot skills.

And probably the most important aspect of our interaction with robots and other very clever machines will be the enhancement of human intelligence.

How important is it to you to erase the boundary between

the viewer and the work, prodding the audience into the role of active, invested participant in the aLife of these robots?

So far my focus point has been "taking the human out of the loop", but the interaction between machines and humans is also an interesting field. Nevertheless, I don't see interaction as human control over the machine but rather as a kind of dialogue between equals, a matter that neither robots nor humans are yet prepared for. Most of the current interaction between humans and machines is a one way process. I am not interested in that, and certainly not in art. If there is any novelty in my projects, it stems from the fact that I don't see the machine as a tool, but as an author.

What are you currently working on?

As an artist I want to disseminate the concept of the Robotarium. As an artist/scientist I am developing a new system of painting robots adding specialization to a swarm of heterogeneous robots to see what happens...

EMERGENCE OF CREATIVE MACHINES [2013]

1. A complex system cannot be understood by examining its individual parts. For a complex system to produce "something" emergent properties must be present. By "something" we understand a recognizable behavior, form or pattern in the mind of the observer. The extension of this recognition, given the state of contemporary knowledge, exceeds now largely what is usually called the visible world. The very small, like molecules or DNA, to the very big, like distant galaxies or black holes, are now objective parts of our world although we cannot see them at the level of our perceptive organs. Our world is expanded.

This kind of expansion doesn't affect only perception. It changes cognition. Emergence is a property of some systems that produce a higher order, a whole, based on the interaction of its simple parts. It demonstrates "how things work" beyond the simplistic mechanics of cause/effect or the linearity of procedures. Actually, emergence is the main mechanism of natural phenomena.

2. In 2003 I have created the first swarm of autonomous robots able to produce original abstract paintings based on emergent behavior. Each robot was equipped with two RGB color detection sensors, four IR obstacle avoidance sensors, a microcontroller and two actuators, one for locomotion and the other for pen manipulation. The microcontroller was an on-board chip, to which the program containing the rules linking the sensors to the actuators was uploaded.

The collective behavior of the set of robots evolving in a canvas (the terrarium that limited the space of the experience), was governed by the gradual increase of the deviation-amplifying feedback mechanism, and the progressive decrease of the random action, until the latter was practically completely eliminated. During the process the robots showed an evident behavior change as the result of the "appeal" of color, triggering a kind of excitement not observed during the initial phase characterized by a random walk.

This was due to the stigmergic interaction, where one robot in fact reacted to what other robots have done. According to Grassé (1959), stigmergy is the production of certain behaviors in agents as a consequence of the effects produced in the local environment by a previous action of other agents. Thus, the collective behavior of the robots was based on randomness, stigmergy and emergence.

3. The results of these experiments demonstrate that autonomous machines can produce a new kind of art. This new kink of art is nonhuman in essence, as once the human operator triggers the process he loses control on the outcome. The absence of conscience, external control or predetermination, allow creative machines to engender creativity in its pure state, without any representational, aesthetic or moral flavor.

The essential of these creations is based on the machine own interpretation of the world and not on its human description. No previous plan, fitness, aesthetical taste or artistic model is induced. These are machines dedicated to their art.

4. In another approach a mesh of a 3d sphere was transformed freely by a mix of algorithms and in some cases an "ant algorithm". The initial shape went through a set of unexpected and radical changes. Holes and spikes appeared deformations occurred. At a given moment the process was stopped and the output sent to a 3d printing machine. A while after an original sculpture was delivered.

The essential of this work is done by machines. My role consists in starting and finishing the process. It may seem very important and some will see it as the inspired touch, the moment of "true" creation, but in fact it can easily be automated. We can imagine a chain of machines creating and printing continuously original sculptures without human intervention.

5. Humans and machines have a common history. We can regard a sharp stone in the hands of the Paleolithic man as a machine to make engravings and trigger abstract thought. Or, consider the Camera obscura, used by renaissance artists, as a machine to enhance realism and perform optical effects. However, today we have a new kind of machines that are more than mere tools. They are creative.

With the advances on artificial intelligence and bio-inspired mechanics we can now state that some machines have a "will" on their own. They produce things that were not pre-determined in the algorithms nor assigned in the application design. In fact, a combination of stochastic processes and emergent behaviors can generate novelty.

This changes radically the role of humans in a creative process when cooperating with machines, be it a simple computer or a sophisticated robot. The cooperation man/machine is of a symbiotic kind, stemming from a constant interaction and successive positive/negative feedbacks from both associates. The human triggers processes but is no longer the exclusive author of the outcome. Hence, concepts need a reevaluation. What means authorship in this new symbiotic context? Shouldn't we redefine art when machines are also creative?

6. Recent years demonstrates a divide between the old humanistic vision that puts the human at the center of all things and the increasing machine autonomy. We witness an effective resistance to the unavoidable cultural change. However, the endeavor to make machines more intelligent, creative and even capable of some consciousness, is determined by need and is now unstoppable. We need that machines become partners and not just obedient slaves. This implies a change in machine skills but above all in human behavior. We need to upgrade our own contribution to the creative process. More than to do things we must concentrate in doing what does. More than to manufacture we should focus on processes that generate an autonomous and unexpected production.

7. Art is an exceptional field for the application of these ideas. Art is experimental by nature. Architecture is another important ground for change. Architecture is artificial by nature. Architecture is synthetic and increasingly determined by the extraordinary capacities of visualization and inventiveness of machines. In particular 3D programs generate new visions impossible to achieve by traditional means. And today digital fabrication, such as in 3D printing, is able to build directly physical spaces.

An agenda for architecture should therefore be inscribed in a wider vision of the new conditions for creativity in the time of the emergence of Creative Machines.

In conclusion I propose 3 principles for a new creativity.
1. Embrace a symbiotic relationship with machines.
2. Explore the power of imagination of machines.
3. Combine all creative processes generate by humans, other life forms and machines.

A NEW KIND OF ART
[2014]

Introduction

We start working with robots as art performers around the turn of the century. Other artists/researchers in the realm of art/technology interface have done similar experiments [1], and their endeavours were a stimulating potency to our work.

After the first trials relying on a bioinspired ant algorithm [2] running on a computer connected to a robotic arm, we decided to focus our research effort on the autonomy of the machine, i.e., the possibility for a machine to create its own drawings and paintings as a kind of artificial creativity stemming from artificial intelligence.

Along these lines, Artsbot, a swarm of art producing robots engendered in 2003 [3] (and updated up to the present time), demonstrates that an interrelated group of robots can generate unique compositions that are independent from the human agent that starts the process.

To the best of our knowledge, Artsbot is the first experiment where robotic art is understood as an emergent process based on a swarm of robots animated by a bioinspired algorithm. By losing control over the output human creators can concentrate on 'making the artists that make the art' [4].

It is worth noting that such machines should not be seen as mere tools or devices for human predetermined aesthetic creations, since they are (at least) partially autonomous and the result of their actions is unpredictable. In addition, although randomness is an essential component of the process, the resulting artwork cannot be viewed as a mere random outcome, given that recognizable patterns emerge [5] from a fuzzy background.

The claim that the compositions produced by Artsbot represent a new kind of art – the art of semi-autonomous machines – may seem controversial in the context of main stream concepts

With Henrique Garcia Pereira

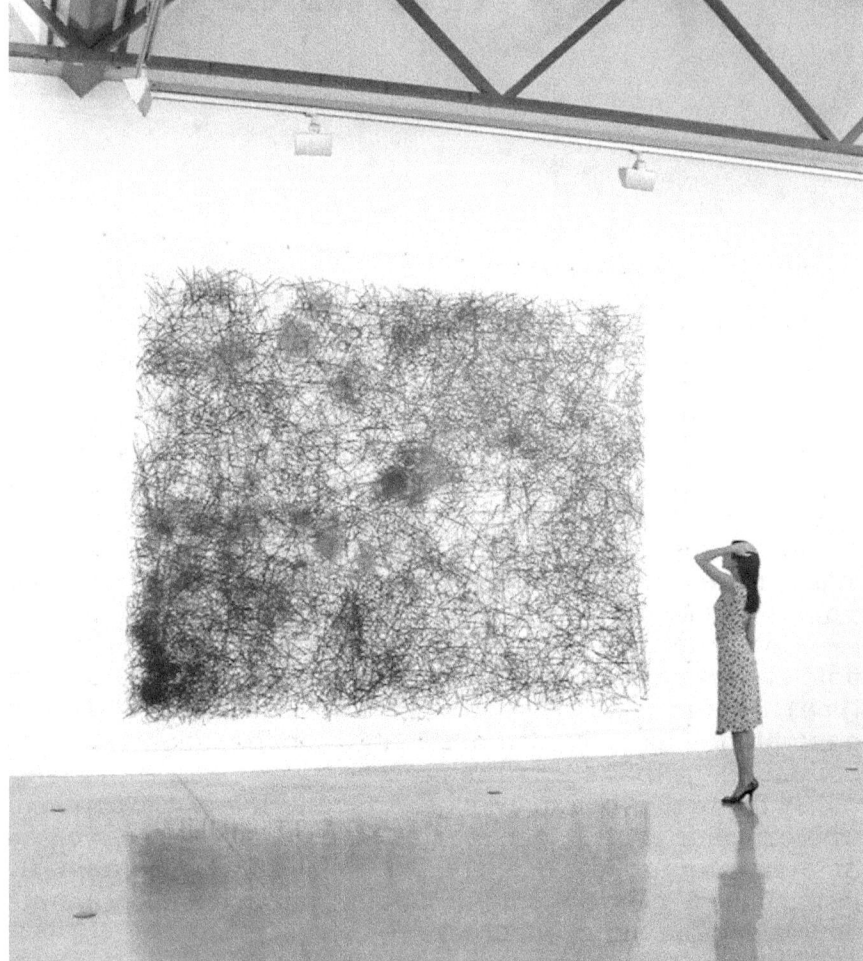

Large painting displayed at an Art Gallery, 2004

that consider art as an exclusive capacity of humans. But, actually, the underlying approach that drives this new kind of art is inscribed in the global advancement of robotics and artificial intelligence towards a greater autonomy of machines. Indeed, as usual, Art simply announces what is about to come.

Machine Art

With the rise of computers, Digital Art was the product of an artificial "language" used to implement routines, trigger behaviours and run algorithms inside machines. The use of computers to make art was initially a subsidiary product of this new language. Artists used computers to generate processes and images that relate mainly to the inner architecture of the machines. Through rules, protocols and algorithms, computers create processes and images as the result of complex calculations.

With the advent of machines as thinking devices able to perform tasks based on their own discretion, a particular form of intelligence coined artificial intelligence was developed, and "computer art" took a new turn, in which complexity is ubiquitous.

Complexity gave rise to the possibility to simulate bioinspired and emergent artificial systems. Hence it was possible to originate what is now known as artificial life, that is, organisms that live inside machines or explore the real world in the form of autonomous sensing robots.

In 2003, from this fresh field of research, we proposed the adjustment of the principles of artificial life to the production of art works by a swarm of autonomous robots (Artsbot). We claim this endeavour to be a new kind of art because a) human creators deliberately lose control over their creations; b) machines, when animated by a particular kind of swarm intelligence, generate a creativity of their own.

Technical description of each Artsbot robot

The basic architecture of each Artsbot robot contains three components: the sensors, the controller and the actuators. The sensors receive signals from the environment, which are processed by the microcontroller in order to command the actuators.

The RGB colour sensors, situated under the robot, can detected the entire palette of colours, but, due to the fact that Artsbot robots carry only two pens, colour detection is divided in just two ranges, Warm and Cold [6]. Proximity sensors assist robots to determine the area of the terrarium [7] and to avoid collisions.

The actuators consist of three servomotors, two for the wheels and one to operate the pens. The controller is an onboard PIC.

Collective behaviour

The case to be made by the proposed approach is that creativity emerges in the set of robots as a consequence of self-organization, driven by their interaction with the environment. Actually, the random walk of each robot – which occurs when the process starts – is only interrupted by the "appeal" of a certain colour spot, trace or patch previously left in the canvas by another robot. Given that the robot only 'sees' a limited region of the canvas, if no colour is detected in that region, it follows its way, putting down a mark of its passage on the canvas only if its random number generator produces a value that exceeds a given threshold. In statistics language, each one of the outcomes of the experiment is regarded as the realisation of a Random Function (RF). The RF is defined as the infinite set of dependent random variables $Z(u)$, one for each location u in a certain area A. In this case, the area A is the canvas, and the random variable is discrete, taking only three nominal colour values – "Warm", "Cold" and "White". The underlying feedback process leads to the spatial dependency of the random variables and explains why clusters are usually formed in most of the RF realisations. These realisations (paintings) are the mapping of the RF onto the canvas, depicting its hybrid structural/random constitutive fundamental nature.

The collective behaviour of the set of robots evolving in a canvas (the terrarium that limits the space of the experience), is governed by the gradual increase of the deviation-amplifying feedback mechanism that is the core of the program governing the controller.

During the process, the robots show an evident behaviour change as a result of the "appeal" of colour, triggering a kind of "excitement" – which can be seen as a bifurcation – that does not occur during the initial phase corresponding to the random walk. Once a robot "sees" a trace of a given colour – classified into the above defined two classes ("warm" and "cold") – the pen of the same colour class is dropped by the corresponding actuator, and consequently this colour class is accentuated in the vicinity of the trace that was previously left in the canvas [8]. As the interaction between robots is not direct, but it is driven by the positive feedback mechanism triggered by a signal left in the environment (this signal makes that the robot turns towards the direction defined by the point where its sensor has detected the colour corresponding to the received signal), we can posit that what is occurring when one robot reacts to what other robots have previously done in the terrarium is a stigmergetic [9] interaction between the robots.

In fact, when developing Artsbot, we have tried to reproduce artificially an emergent behaviour "similar" to the natural behaviour of ants, bees, termites, and other social insects. These insects communicate among themselves through chemical messages, the pheromones, with which they produce certain patterns of collective behaviour, like follow a trail, clean up, repair and build nests, defense and attack or territory conquest. Despite pheromone is not the exclusive way of communication among these insects – the touch of antennas in ants or the dance in bees are equally important –, pheromonal language produces complex cognition via bottom-up procedures. As previously stated, this procedure is obviously an indirect form of communication, coined stigmergy by Grassé, from the Greek stigma/sign and ergon/action.

Following these principles, we have "replaced" pheromone by colour. The marks left by one robot triggers a pictorial action on other robot, without any direct relation between them. Through this pseudo random mechanism, abstract paintings are generated, revealing well defined shapes and patterns. Artsbot creates abstract paintings that seem at first sight just random doodles, but – after some reflexive observation – colour clusters and patterns become patent. Through the recognition of the coloured marks left by a robot, the others react to it reinforcing certain colour spots. The process is thus everything but arbitrary.

Actually, what is crucial in the Artsbot experiment is the concept of emergence applied to a process that drives the swarm behaviour. Indeed, in the swarm behaviour, emergence arises when multiple agents, which interact with each other and the environment in a rather haphazardly way, may generate order as a consequence of some form of swarm intelligence [10]. The process by which these mechanics can produce a novel behaviour (quasi-) independent of the human that implements and starts the process cannot be analytically modelled, but it should be understood as producing a new gestalt, along the lines of the complex dynamic theory (known commonly as "theory of chaos").

For some authors, emergence is just a deterministic mechanism. According to this view, the set of rules or initial conditions determines the behaviour, and unpredictability is an emergent property of a system that may be predictable on a lower level of analysis. But, since any complex system cannot be understood by examining its individual parts [11], we claim that the deterministic view underestimates important components of the emergent process that is the backbone of the collective behaviour produced by Artsbot.

Discussion and conclusion

In our approach the human artist creates the process but not the resulting drawing or painting [12]. Although the set of rules is changeable according to certain parameters, the most determining component of the process lies on the fact that the robots are driven by the data they gather from the environment.

In Artsbot, our Painting Robots were designed to paint (not a specific painting but their own paintings). Their creations stem from the machine own interpretation of the world and not from its human description. No previous plan, fitness, aesthetic taste or artistic model is brought about. Our robots are machines dedicated to their art.

With the new advances in neurobiology, intelligence is understood as a basic feedback mechanism. If a system, any system, is able to respond to a certain stimulus in a way that it changes itself or its environment, we can state that some sort of intelligence is present. "Sheer" intelligence is therefore something that does not need to refer to any kind of purpose, target or quantification. It may be plainly an interactive mechanism of any kind, with no other objective than to process information and to react in accordance to available input characteristics.

Although the starting point of Artsbot was bioinspiration (in particular, modelling social insect's emergent behaviour), its basic idea has evolved to constructing machines able to generate a new kind of art with a minimum of fitness constraints, optimization parameters or real life simulation. In this sense, we are not so much concerned with manufacture overcoming, but with taking the human out of the loop. The statement that machines can make art have implications far beyond the simple machine ability to mimic human behaviour. It opens the concept of art to all kinds of living forms, natural and artificial.

_____

1. Since the sixties of last century, with cybernetic art and the works by Nam June Paik, Jean Tinguely and others, artists used machines and later robots in order to produce art. Some were just mechanical devices, but with the proliferation of computers they become more and more "intelligent" and increasingly autonomous. For an informed approach to the history of art and robots see

Eduardo Kac's "Origin and development of robotic art" <http://www.ekac.org/roboticart.html>

2. This algorithm, coined ACO (Ant Colony Optimization), was developed by Marco Dorigo in 1992 in his PhD thesis.

3. The first results of the Artsbot project, as well as its rationale and underlying process, are reported in Moura, L. and Pereira, H.G. , Man+Robots, Symbiotic Art, (Villeurbane, France: Institut d'Art Contemporain, Collection Écrits d'artistes, 2004)

4. Symbiotic Art Manifesto, 2004 <http://www.leonelmoura.com/manifesto.html>   89

5. The concept of emergence as we view it is comprehensively addressed by Johnson, S, Emergence: The Connected Lives of Ants, Brains, Cities, and Software (New York : Scribner, 2001)

6. In our work, colour is the analogue to pheromone in ants.

7. The terrarium is the area where the set of robots travels, executing the action of painting through the interdependence of their paths. It consists of a canvas laying on a horizontal surface, bounded by small (10 cm) vertical white walls that limit the space where robots can move.

8. This procedure is analogue to the case made by Herbert Simon, when he describes the situation in which a moving agent reinforces known paths, once previous choices have proved satisfying, as put forward in Simon, H., The sciences of the artificial, (Cambridge, Mass.; London: MIT Press, 1996).

9. Stigmergy is the production of certain behaviours in agents as a consequence of the effects produced in the local environment by a previous action of other agents. It worth noting that the biologist P. P. Grassé was the first researcher to develop this concept in the scope of his study of social insects behaviour, as reported in Grassé , P. P. 'La réconstruction du nid et les coordinations inter-individuelles chez Bellicositermes Natalienses et cubitermes sp. La théorie de la stigmergie: Essai d'interpretation des termites constructeurs', Ins. Soc., 6, p. 41-48, 1959.

10. This concept was developed by Eric Bonabeau, Marco Dorigo and Guy Theraulaz, Swarm Intelligence, (New York: Oxford: Oxford University Press, 1999).

11. This a point sharply made by Daniel Dennett, on the basis of his concept of intentional emergence as the main property of complex systems. This concept is developed in Dennett, D., 'Intentional systems theory', in Inside Art and Science, (Lisbon: LxXL, 2009) p. 58-81.

12. This assertion embraces the approach discussed in Shanken, E. 'Art in information age: Technology and conceptual art', in Invisible College: Reconsidering "Conceptual Art" (Cambridge: Ed. by Michael Corris, Cambridge UP, 2001)

COMBINING EMERGENCE AND CONTROL (2014)

The breakthrough brought about by the predictable evolution of 3D print-ers opens the possibility to "print" entire buildings in the future. Such a task will mainly be performed by machines and industrial robots under a strict software control as it happens today in most factories.

To achieve a right end-product, accuracy is a crucial requirement. Hence, these 3D printers will be very sophisticated but mere reproductive tools.

Though, we can imagine a new kind of machines able to "create" architec-tural plans and, at the same time, putting them into practice. Those machines can generate innovation and novelty based on trial and error, self-organization and, above all, emergence. Given the particular features of architectural ob-jects, some control is however needed in the entire process. Buildings have doors, windows, stairs, specific volumes and many other constraints.

Our experience with a new kind of art produced by robots able to create original paintings based on emergent processes show the possibility to apply Bioinspired emergent processes to art and architecture.

For architecture however a combination of emergence and control may contribute to approach this problem from a new angle. Some hints are given in this paper on this issue.

3D printing

3D printing is currently undergoing an impressive expan-sion, which has enlarged enormously its use, since the 1980s. Novel machines, processes and materials are being swiftly pro-duced and offered to the common consumer at a reasonable cost. 3D printers are becoming just another printer indispens-able in any office, and soon in every home.

Using a x, y, z grid as reference, such machines manufac-ture 3D objects by operating layer by layer a given material, which is the analogue of the "ink" in conventional printers. In contrast to the milling processes, which remove material from a block, 3D printing adds it.

Obviously, the thinner is the layer, the more accurate the outcome. Still, what really makes it possible to undertake these new constructions are the specific qualities of the basic mate-rial, which needs to be something able to alter promptly its mo-

With Henrique Garcia Pereira, first published in Next Generation Building 1/2014, Baltzer Science Publishers

lecular structure, from soft to hard. From polymers to chocolate, anything that can solidify quickly may serve as printing matter.

The proliferation of machines and uses is accelerating the 3D printers evolutionary process, in a way similar to the Internet exponential (and contagious) growth. Clearly, more users stimulate innovation. In addition to experiments with new materials, nylon or salt for example, users seem to be interested in objects with bigger and bigger size. The first and until now most common printing machines deliver small objects, whose dimensions are, in general, hardly bigger than a hand. For this order of magnitude, a problem can arise when extreme accuracy is needed. For the substantial majority of large objects, as a vehicle, a chair or a wall of a house, sufficient accuracy is easily achieved, provided that the model is properly designed.

Te possibility of printing an entire building is no more a science fiction vision. Nowadays, several architects and schools are actively working on this theme. Apart from economic questions, this approach increases significantly the architect's autonomy, since he/she produces his/her building blocks (in the literal sense) from scratch, which eliminates the separation between architect and builder. Also, the trial and error process is facilitated by this way of connecting design and construction.

Control

Control is defined, in the context of this paper, basically as a set of instructions that make a machine perform previous determined tasks. This can be done in a linear fashion, such as a "go to" or a "do this or that" instructions suggest. It can also include positive or negative feedback, as when a threshold parameter is introduced, or when an "if then" line of code induces a response to a condition "observed" by the machine by means of sensors. For example, the heater of our house is automatically switched off when a room reaches a certain temperature (the pre-defined threshold), and it is switched again on, when it gets colder.

Such a kind of autonomy may seem casual but is in fact rigorously controlled.

Control is defined by the action leading to a predetermined purpose, measured by the exactness of the machine performance. Any deviation is considered a loss of control.

This means that, although a machine behavior can be quite complex and astonishing, it just reproduces a written script. Control operates in opposition to creativeness and originality. Machines under control reproduce over and over exactly the same tasks.

Emergence

Machines can be creative when they are allowed to have some discretionary behavior, that is, a type of behavior which is not driven by any set of pre-defined rules. A very basic form of machine discretionary behavior derives from the way information is gathered. When all the information regarding a certain problem is previously uploaded to the machine, there is no way for it to behave differently from the course of action induced by the set of instructions obtainable from such complete information. But if the machine is able to gather and process information through its sensors, that is, gathering novel information, then behavior can change to the point that it cannot be predicted.

In addition to the obvious interaction with the environment generated by response to sensors, it is also important to consider the interaction with other agents, as well as with previous actions preserved in a kind of stigmergic memory. This type of behavior cannot be governed by preset rules. On the other hand, results of such a behavior vis-à-vis a whole is obviously superior to the sum of the parts, since all components of the system, including environmental elements, are conceptualized as being capable of agency. Emergence can produce control if interaction between the parts is applied to the constraints itself, to properties or to threshold variation.

For emergent design in an architectural scenario, primitive level investigations pursue distinct realms – such as morphology, materials and structure – by using a bottom up methodology. These investigations are subsequently integrated and non-linearly combined to shape the architectural experience. The solution derived from such a methodology based on a decentralized style of thinking is advantageous because it has the flexibility to be revised in any aspect appropriate to change, or in a new understanding of the design scenario.

Emergent design leads to chaotic systems in which patterns are recognizable, in a context whose analogies with natural form and organic growth are striking. In particular, these analogies stem from the insight for understanding how complex, collective, macroscopic phenomena arise from simple, local interaction of individuals (or basic elements of a system).

Termite cathedrals

Termites are social insects. They reproduce, live and behave in a collective environment. However, unlike (some?) human communities, termites don't act under the drive of a central coordination, command or leadership. The Queen, whose name can be misleading, is the reproductive organ of the colony. It emits pheromone messages in order to be taken care of, but it does not determine the individual behavior of termites in their daily activities. Social behavior is self-organized and the whole can be regarded as a superorganism (Hölldobler & Wilson, 2009).

In termite world "architecture" is an essential task. The nest is not only the site for survival, providing shelter and defense from predators, but is also the organizing system of nourishment, behavior, interaction and actually, existence of each individual and the community as a whole.

Nest construction is the way termites evolved to "modulate reality" (Sadler, 1999).

The mound is the visible part of the nest. It functions as a shaft for the underground "cellar". The whole nest consists of a complex system of chambers, tunnels, conduits for ventilation in a wide range of shapes and sizes. The structure is homeostatic and sustainable.

Made of local materials, with a porosity and mechanical strength similar to adobe bricks, it shows a remarkable capacity of adaptation to external conditions and attacks.

The crucial point of the construction mechanism used by termites is based on a combination of pheromone stimulus and gravity. Termites begin by sticking small round pellets embedded with pheromone which stimulates the continuity of the operation. After a while, the assembly of pellets becomes pillars, and at a given moment, these bend under the gravitational force. If these tilting pillars encounter a facing one, an arch is formed. If not, the procedure starts all over again.

The process is of a trial and error kind, self-organized and emergent.

A new kind of art

A "Swarm Sculpture", 2000, was created by an Artificial Life algorithm in the computer and later casted in Plexiglas. A swarm of artificial ants were launched in the continuous space of a tridimensional sphere, subdivided in a grid of regular cells.

The artificial pheromone deposition and evaporation of the "ants" produced a positive or negative displacement of the cells generating the deformation of the sphere, where more pheromone results in peaks and less in valleys. After a certain number of iterations the initial space was transformed in a sculptural body.

After this experience we felt the need to remove the intermediary human element, from computer to physical, and opt for robotics. In 2003 a swarm of small robots were able to create original paintings based on Bioinspired multi-agent interaction (Moura & Pereira, 2004). Each robot reacted to previous inputs, color marks, left by other robots in a stigmergic fashion. The results are paintings with distinct patterns which, at the level of perception, simulate a compositional attempt.

Swarm paintings demonstrate the possibility to develop a new kind of art based on artificial creativity, were the human is a triggering device in an emergent and out-of control process. Constraints are defined by the arena space, detected by the robots trough the use of obstacle sensors, and parameter thresholds for color evaluation with RGB sensors.

The main information for reactive and stigmergic behavior is gathered by each robot itself and cannot be previously uploaded.

The construction of such paintings is analogous to the described termite procedures.

From an initial random action perceptible forms emerge.

Neuromorphic computing

Even though Artificial Life (ALife) – as coined by Langton (2000) for the machine biomimicricy of social insects (applied to Swarm Intelligence, cf. Bonabeau, Dorigo, & Theraulaz, 1999) – gave rise to important practical outcomes in the 20th century, a new and richer approach is arising in recent years. Instead of using colonies of social insects as a model for inspiring analogies for autonomous machine design, the new approach – denoted 'neuromorphic computing' – tries to mimic what happens in human brain.

However, this approach suffers from a serious drawback: we don't understand but a small fraction of human brain performance (pessimistic expert guesses estimate such fraction in 1%). None less, in the next decades, it is expected that such a drawback can be (partially?) overcame by formidable (and costly) Research Projects launched in Europe and USA (Boddhu, 2012). The aim of these projects is to produce machines that have some characteristics that brains have and computers have not. These are: lower power consumption (while human brain uses about 20 watts, supercomputers currently used to try to simulate it need several megawatts); fault tolerance (loosing just one transistor can wreck a microprocessor, but brains loose neurons all the time); and a lack of need to be programmed (brains learn as they interact with the world, instead of following the fixed path of a predetermined algorithms). The method by which these aims can be approached relies on analogue computers, which are re-appearing again because they operate in a way closer to some features of a real nervous system. Furthermore, their speed is much greater than the corresponding value for digital ones, providing an exciting picture of the "society of mind" vision, as anticipated by Marvin Minsky, a 'Founder Father' of Artificial Intelligence.

Emergent control?

If machines ought to start printing buildings using extended 3D printing techniques that include ALife concepts stemming from mimicry (based on termite colonies behavior or – in the future – on human brain models), two distinct processes can be envisaged: the first depends on Control and the second follows the Out of control paradigm, as put forward by Kevin Kelly, summarized in his drastic statement: "Whenever the word emergent appears, there disappears human control" (Kelly, 1994, p. 30).

Totally controlled machines will be reproducing a previous plan that can replicate endlessly.

They will look and behave like industrial robots. Even in the case in which the rules of "optimal design" (Papalambros & Wilde, 1988) are applied, this process will lead to architectural outcome that does no qualitatively differ from the ones produced by 'classical' planning.

The other alternative is to let the machine build its own architectural object. In this case, the plan is not detached from the construction. Actually it emerges from it, and replication is not possible. The machine will be producing different forms each time.

This choice poses some problems, even though the dichotomy is not completely clear cut. In fact, even Kevin Kelly concedes that control may co-evolve with emergence by the extensive use of stacked feed-back loops (Kelly, 1994, p. 154–164).

Apart from economic and ecological considerations, the constructions produced by this new kind of architecture must contemplate some basic elements, like structural constraints. On the other hand, such constructions must have a purpose, defined by the 'client', and must comply with local conditions of the ground surface on which they are to be erected.

We argue that this set of constraints can be integrated in the emergent process through a method that expands, by amplified biomimicracy, the system above outlined for termites, in their arch building technique. As E.O. Wilson noted "the history of termites can be viewed as a slow escape by means of architectural innovation from a dependence of rotting wood for shelter". (Wilson, 1971, p. 315).

In our approach, extended to neuromorphic computing, the two above delineated alternatives can be merged into one, by generating some kind of control over the output of the emergent process. Such a control may be based on cellular automata algorithms, along the lines of Wolfram (2002). In fact, the space where the emergent process evolves can be 'compelled' to comply with the requested properties by imposing a probabilistic rule. These proprieties can be seen as the analogue of the 'attractors' that drive bottom up a non-linear dynamic system, leading to patterns in an apparently chaotic context.

Imagine a tridimensional space as a set of points each evolving from an emergent process. If the causal interaction between the points is defined by simple rules triggering patterns of behavior, like is the case in cellular automata, it is possible to generate some kind of control over the output. This space would be build by the subset of points with higher probability to establish relationships.

The role of the architect of the future is not to make plans, but to conceive building processes that can generate some controlled output through an emergence based process.

Boddhu, S. K. (2012). Qualitative functional decomposition analysis of evolved neuromorphic flight controllers.
Applied Computational Intelligence and Soft Computing, 2.
Bonabeau, E., Dorigo, M., & Theraulaz, G. (1999). Swarm intelligence. New York, NY: Oxford University Press.
Hölldobler, B., & Wilson, E. O. (2009). The super-organism. New York, NY: W.W. Norton.
Kelly, K. (1994). Out of control. London: Forth Estate.
Langton, C. G. (2000). Artificial life, an overview. Cambridge, MA: MIT.
Moura, L., & Pereira, H. G. (2004). Man1robots symbiotic art. Villeurbanne: Institut d'Art Contemporain.
Papalambros, P., & Wilde, D. (1988). Principles of optimal design. Cambridge, MA: Cambridge University Press.
Sadler, S. (1999). The situationist city. Cambridge, MA: MIT.
Wilson, E. O. (1971). Insect societies. Cambridge, MA: Belknap.
Wolfram, S. (2002). A new kind of science. Champaign, IL: Wolfram Media.